MIND YOUR MANNERS

An Etiquette Guide for Youth and Young Adults

Written and Illustrated by

Edwardlene Fleeks Willis, Ph.D.

© 1997, 2002 by Edwardlene Fleeks Willis, Ph.D.
All rights reserved.

No part of this book may be reproduced, stored in a retrieval system, or transmitted by any means, electronic, mechanical, photocopying, recording, or otherwise, without written permission from the author.

ISBN: 0-7596-5848-X (Softcover)
ISBN: 0-7596-5847-1 (Ebook)

This book is printed on acid free paper.

1stBooks - rev. 8/08/02

TABLE OF CONTENTS

INTRODUCTION..vii

I. **MIND YOUR MANNERS** 1
Definition...Customs... Good Manners and Others...

II. **GOOD MANNERS AT HOME**........................5
Privacy... Borrowing... Self-Control... Neatness...
Checklist... Telephone Etiquette... Cell Phone...
Etiquette...Curfews... Dating... Personal...
Responsibility...

III. **GOOD MANNERS AT SCHOOL** 13
How to Get Along at School... Checklist...
The Cafeteria... School Corridors... Auditorium...
Tips...Making Friends...Personal Appearance...
School Clothes...

IV. **PARTY MANNERS**...................................... 20
Party Strategies...Formal Dances...Formal Clothes...
Corsages...Calling for Your Date...Dance Cards...
Subscription Dances...and Stag Line...
Refusing a Dance

V. **ENTERTAINING** 28
Invitations... Being a Good Host/Hostess...
Refreshments... Setting the Table...
Table Manners... Buffet Supper... Equipment and
Supplies... Having fun at Parties...

VI.	DATING ETIQUETTE 43

Getting a Date...Accepting a Date...
Dressing for a Date... Having a Good Date...
Conversing With Others... Having Blind Dates...
Restraunt Rules... Going Steady... Breaking Up...
Ending a Date...

VII.	HOW TO BEHAVE IN PUBLIC 56

At the Movies... Attending a performance... Arriving After a Performance Begins... Watching a Performance... Attending Athletic Events... Visiting a Church... Going Shopping... Riding in a Vehicle... Riding an Elevator... Riding an Escalator...
Smoking, Alhohol and Drugs

VIII.	GENERAL TIPS ON ETIQUETTE 69

Introductions... Correspondence... Electronic-Mail System... Voice-Mail System... Voice-Mail Etiquette... Weekending Driving Manners...
Cellular Phone Driving Tips...

IX.	BUSINESS ETIQUETTE 81

Applying for a Job... The Interview... Keeping a Job... Baby Sitting

X.	TRAVEL ETIQUETTE AND TIPS 92

Planning and Preparing for Your Trip... (Travel Agents)... Method of Payment... Insurance... Travel Documents... Medical and Health Considerations...

Customs and Taxes... In Flight Tips... Cruise Planning... Selecting A Cruise... Cabins and Staterooms... Dining at Sea... Dress and Special Events... Tipping... Vocabulary of the Sea... Before Leaving Reading... Foreign Language Guidebook... Travel Journal/Diary... Packing... Packing Lists... Things To Do Before Leaving... Bartering...

XI.   **SUMMARY** 116

      INDEX 117

INTRODUCTION

This book was written especially for youth and young adults who need some suggestions about what to do when they face uncomfortable situations at home, school, in public, and in the workplace. It is also a response to questions asked of me as a mother, former public school teacher and principal, and as a volunteer for several community organizations.

Knowing how to solve the special problems that we face in our everyday lives by "doing the right thing", at the right lime helps us to feel good about ourselves. Consequently, it helps us to develop good relationships with others.

"Mind your manners" is a statement often made to young people as they are growing up. "Where are your manners?" is the question often asked after someone interrupts a conversation, slurps soup or slams a door. To avoid getting upset about things like this or worry about them, treat others, as you want to be treated and use a little common sense. These are the basics needed for practicing good manners.

Mind Your Manners
An Etiquette Guide for Youth and Young Adults

CHAPTER I

MIND YOUR MANNERS

Manners tell a lot about a person. Practicing good manners helps to open the doors to self-improvement and an understanding of others. Therefore, they are important. You want your manners to tell the best things about you—the real, considerate, intelligent person you really are. It seems unfair, but often a person's intelligence and kindness are overlooked because of bad manners. To be liked and accepted among people world-wide, certain customs must be practiced. These are known as etiquette or good manners.

Definition

Etiquette is defined as the conduct or procedures established by custom as acceptable or required in society, a profession or in official life. Simply, etiquette is a combination of strict rules and easy good manners. Rules are learned either by trial-and-error, observation, or by using a book of etiquette to look up specific problems. Good manners, common sense combined with thoughtfulness for others, are perhaps the most important ingredients of etiquette.

Edwardlene Fleeks Willis, Ph.D.

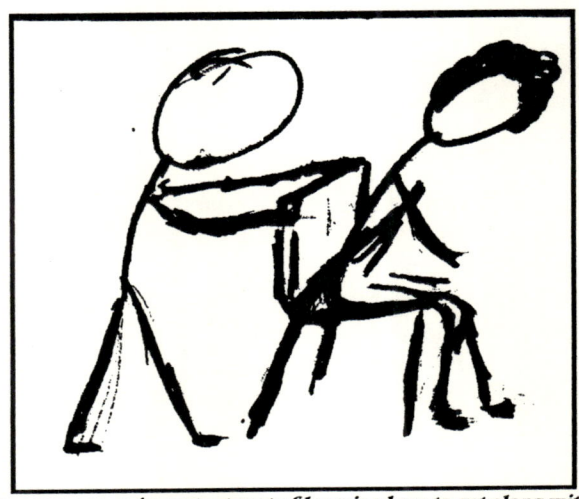

(Good manners are an important part of learning how to get along with others.)

Custom

Etiquette is partly a series of customs that society develops to serve specific purposes. Customs vary from country to country and from generation to generation. Customs that seem "right" to some people seem "wrong" to others. For example, in the United States shaking hands is the custom when meeting people. Asian cultures think this is strange. They consider it a mark of respect to bow. To each country, its own customs mean correct behavior. When visiting other countries, it is a good idea to be familiar with their customs or standards of behavior.

Customs change through the years. In the U. S., at one time it was considered extremely impolite for a gentleman to remain seated while a lady stood. Although in social situations this is still true, it has become common custom for women to stand on subways and buses; only on rare occasions does a man offer his seat to a woman. This is one of the changes that have occurred as woman's place in American society has changed.

Many old customs have remained although their original purpose has disappeared. Why is it "correct" for a man to walk on the outside of the sidewalk? Originally, that was to protect the lady from being splashed by a passing carriage. Men's coats are made to open on the right because years ago a man had to be able to draw his sword (which hung on the right side) quickly.

Many customs are followed in church service, weddings, or formal dinners. They are usually rules of procedures that make the particular occasion run smoothly. Knowing all the rules and being able to spot an oyster fork at first glance or cope with a finger bowl isn't enough. You need to have easy good manners always and under all circumstances.

Good Manners and Others

There are many do's and don'ts about etiquette, but being pleasant and considerate of others is the most important rule to remember. Pulling out a chair or holding open a door, are little things that show you are thinking of others. Good manners should grow with you, from your earliest years. They should be natural, not something you turn on and off like a light switch. They should be used everyday. Some people have two sets of manners - company manners and everyday manners. This can be embarrassing. If careless of your manners at home, you may one day find your hostess staring while you talk with a full mouth and wave your fork around for added emphasis. Make "company manners" your everyday manners. Then you won't have to worry about remembering the "right thing to do" when you are away from home.

Edwardlene Fleeks Willis, Ph.D.

Everyone makes mistakes. At one time or other, everyone forgets to introduce two strangers, or eats a neighbor's salad. But etiquette is more than following rules. It is confidence in yourself and your attitude toward others. By keeping your poise, you can get through many an uncomfortable situation with ease. Most mistakes seem unimportant or are unnoticed by everyone except you. Never try to cover up an error by a lot of apologies. Just say you are sorry and try to forget the whole thing. Everyone else will.

Good manners play an important part in relationships with your family, friends, teachers, and dates. They can add to your popularity and success. They can smooth your path through life. This booklet was written to help ease some of the bumps in your path and provide tips on getting along better at home, in school, at social affairs, in public, and on the job.

Mind Your Manners
An Etiquette Guide for Youth and Young Adults

CHAPTER II

GOOD MANNERS AT HOME

Home is a wonderful place to relax and be you. At school, visiting, when on a date and everywhere else—you should be at your best. But at home it is easy to unwind and ease into familiar, comfortable surroundings.

This is fine, provided everyone at home practices good manners. No one should take advantage of the love and understanding expected from family members by having two standards of behavior - one for your family and one for others. Good manners around the house are the forerunner of good business and social manners. If you forget the errand Mother asked you to do after school, you are probably going to forget the employer's instructions, too. If you duck kitchen police, cooking in your future will be a major problem instead of the fun it should be. The home is the best place to practice good manners.

Privacy

Each family member needs some privacy. Respect a closed door. Even if a sister is only experimenting with makeup, knock and wait for an answer before barging into the room. Don't be too curious. A family member's mail, bureau drawers, and desks are private. How would you feel if someone rummaged through your things?

(Borrowing from family members too much too often is a bad habit)

Borrowing

Borrowing is often fun, but it can cause trouble, too. To stay on good terms with your friends and family, go easy on the borrowing. It seems simple, when you get bored with your skirts or ties, to help yourself to those of others. But it is hard to explain to someone how you happened to spill ice cream over a favorite outfit of theirs when he or she needs it for a date. Borrowing is a dangerous habit to acquire. It starts with the family and before you realize it you are borrowing in school—a comb, books, and even money for that extra soda. Before long you find yourself facing a cold stare when you start asking for something. Try not to get the habit, and you will never have to break it. Practice the adage, "Neither a borrower nor a lender be."

Self Control

Everyone has gloomy moods. There are days when someone may snap at you unfairly. At school a friend passes you in the hall with hardly a glance, and you fail to get that part in the play you had your heart set on. Control may last just so long and then you arrive home with a long face and a sour disposition. Other family members have had a day of disappointments too, and soon irritations are taken out on each other.

Often there are floods of tears. They should be controlled because tears don't help. It is comforting, at times, to have the family's shoulders to cry on. But it can be overdone. Crying at the drop of a handkerchief can become a habit if you let it. It doesn't usually get you what you want, and it prevents you from doing something constructive about your problem. Everyone has moments when the tears flow in spite of everything. You are upset because you had a fight with a date, or you get a flat "no" to all your pleading for a new outfit, or there may be other reasons. But if you learn to control your tears, you can shed them in private, and avoid distressing everyone around you.

Edwardlene Fleeks Willis, Ph.D.

Neatness

It is usually the little things that bother parents. These can cause the nagging children dislike. Sloppiness is one of those "little things". It shows indifference and laziness. Arriving at the dinner table in a bathrobe and curlers is one form of sloppiness. Using poor table manners and leaving your bed unmade are others. Being tidy takes very little extra time, but what a difference it makes. Here are a few specific things that particularly irritate parents. Check yourself and see how you rate.

Checklist

		Usually	Sometimes	Never
1.	Do you leave a trail of clothes and athletic gear wherever you go?	___	___	___
2.	Do you track mud into the house?	___	___	___
3.	Do you leave recordings on the floor?	___	___	___
4.	Do you leave a ring around the bathtub?	___	___	___
5.	Do you dawdle in the bathroom?	___	___	___
6.	Do you hurry away from the dinner table?	___	___	___
7.	Is your aim at the wastebasket poor?	___	___	___
8.	Do you leave windows open when it is raining?	___	___	___
9.	Do you plant your feet all over the furniture?	___	___	___
10.	Do you expect somebody else to clean up for your guests?	___	___	___

If your answers to all ten questions were in the first column, your Neatness Quotient is pretty low and needs a large amount of boosting. If you check most of the questions in the middle column, you are fairly neat but could spend a little more time and effort on being tidy. If most of your checks landed in the third column, you are the answer to every parent's prayer.

Telephone Etiquette

The telephone is a very important instrument in any house, and it deserves gentle care and treatment. Always answer pleasantly; you never know who is likely to be at the other end of the line. (It may be Mr. Wonderful or Miss Right) Avoid grunts or mumbles. Speak slowly and distinctly and keep your voice friendly, even for wrong numbers. If the call is for someone else, you can say. "May I ask who is calling?" Write down any message—as accurately as possible. There should always be a pad and pencil handy. Everyone likes to have messages remembered or clearly written.

Cell Phone Etiquette Tips

1. Adjust speaker volume on your cell phone during conversations, especially in public.
2. Adjust ringer volume on your cell phone as needed to avoid distractions.
3. Avoid using your cell phone during meals and other situations where regular conversations are underway.

Curfews

The question of the amount of time you may spend unescorted causes trouble in many families. Stretching the curfew, especially on date nights, happens quite often. When parents say midnight is the limit, and you stroll in casually al 1:00 a.m. with a variety of excuses, they are likely to be unpleasant about it. Then you complain that they are treating you Like a child.

(After your parents and you have agreed on a curfew, keep your part of the bargain.)

This situation can be handled with little difficulty. First have a long talk with your parents and come to an agreement you both feel is fair. Second, STICK TO THE AGREEMENT. It may be hard to believe, but parents really worry when children don't make the curfew. Be considerate and get home when expected. Your family life will be much happier.

Dating

There are other aspects of dating besides curfews that call for consideration and thoughtfulness. Give parents a chance to know and like the fellows or girls you want to date. Invite them to your house. If your dates are the people you think they are, parents are sure to like them. Give them the opportunity to meet John or Dorothy, who has just been a name to them.

Remember too, that parents like to have some idea of your plans for a date. Emphasize time, places and persons involved. "Dorothy and I are making the eight o'clock movie and then we are meeting Mark and Keisha for sodas. We will come home right after that." Your willingness to offer it shows real consideration and maturity. It may seem like a small matter to you, but it is important to your parents.

Personal Responsibility

One of the best demonstrations of good manners at home is accepting a certain amount of responsibility - both for you and the family at large. Do you expect Mom to fish out the dirty socks from under the bed? Is the bathroom a mess when you come out? Are you absent when housecleaning is in full swing? Everybody is guilty of such behavior at times. But the considerate, adult individual usually shares in the chores of the house. Boys and girls can learn to make a bed and clean their own rooms. Both can take care of their own clothes. Some females through the ages have tended to pamper men in this respect, but that's no excuse for not hanging your clothes up neatly or pressing your own trousers.

One family found a successful plan for dividing the work of the house. Every month, or so, they have a conference. Mom or Dad gives out a list of all the chores. One by one they are auctioned off, each chore going to the highest bidder. This way, every person chooses a chore and is thereafter responsible for it.

Parents will be impressed if children take the initiative occasionally, and offer to do something special. For example, a daughter could relieve Mom in the kitchen and fix dinner once a week. A son could take care of his brother on a Saturday so Mom and Dad could go on a dale!

Edwardlene Fleeks Willis, Ph.D.

It is a fact—showing good manners and consideration to your family as well as to your friends makes for more pleasant living.

Mind Your Manners
An Etiquette Guide for Youth and Young Adults

CHAPTER III

GOOD MANNERS AT SCHOOL

How to Get Along at School

Many of your waking hours are spent at school. Try to make life there as smooth as possible. Getting along at school involves both your classroom work and relationships with the staff and other students. To get along successfully at school, practice good manners.

Teachers play an important part in school life. How well you get along with them can make all the difference in your success and happiness during classroom hours.

The important thing to remember is that every teacher is a person. All kinds of people teach. Some you will like, some you will dislike. A teacher has problems and responsibilities just like you, and also has "off days". A teacher may be worried about bills or have a toothache, anxious because someone is ill, or annoyed because a few class members are behavior problems or failing in their work. Keep in mind, how well you perform in class affects your teacher, too. A teacher is rated by superiors on how successfully students learn the subject being taught.

Regardless of your personal feelings, treat your teachers with respect and courtesy and try to get to know them. You will find they are interested in your problems and accomplishments and anxious to know and to help you. Teachers are pleased when you grasp their subject and show a real interest in the work. Many are willing to spend time after class to explain a particularly puzzling point, or to help you with a personal problem.

Be attentive in class and really concentrate, instead of daydreaming or gazing out the window. A receptive, alert attitude will reflect in your grades. Do your own schoolwork and accept the responsibility for it. It isn't fair to let your friend do all of your math homework or let your partner do most of the experiments and you get credit you do not deserve. Avoid letting homework assignments pile up and then turning them in late.

Checklist

		YES	NO
1.	Do you make dates and party plans outside the classroom?	___	___
2.	Do you give the boy or girl at the next desk more attention than the teacher?	___	___
3.	Are you prompt for all classes?	___	___
4.	Do you comb your hair or apply cosmetics in class?	___	___
5.	Do you show off at the blackboard?	___	___
6.	Do you think you know all the answers and constantly wave you hands at the teacher?	___	___
7.	When bored in class, do you write personal correspondence or other things unrelated to class activities?	___	___
8.	Do you copy your neighbor's notes because you were inattentive?		
9.	Do you find your desk so confining that you sprawl all over the aisle?	___	___
10.	Are you the class clown joker, always playing around and making wisecracks?	___	___

The Cafeteria

By the time your last morning class is over, lunch is uppermost in your thoughts. That doesn't give you the license to stampede into the cafeteria! Line up quietly and patiently without pushing and shoving. Giving the student in front of you a friendly pat on the head with your tray is kid stuff! Decide what you want to eat quickly and stick to your decision so you won't hold up the line. In some schools, the boys often flock to one end of the cafeteria and the girls congregate at the other end. Being social at lunchtime is a friendly, easy way of getting to know the other sex better. If this happens in you cafeteria, why not try to break up this arrangement? An easy habit to get into is eating lunch every day with the same group. You may be missing the chance to know a lot of interesting people. Too, a new student in school would appreciate a cordial, "Why not sit with us today?" It is the perfect opportunity to introduce a new student to your friends and help the new student to adjust to a new school.

Table manners are for the school cafeteria, too! They will be discussed later. Remember company table manners should be an every day affair.

School Corridors

Corridors have been provided in schools to get students from room to room quickly and quietly. Do not run through the halls, yell to someone al the top of your voice, crash carelessly into people, or obstruct traffic. You may want to chat with friends between classes, but do it briefly and in a normal tone of voice. Corridors are not meant for talk sessions, club meetings or learning the latest dance step.

Edwardlene Fleeks Willis, Ph.D.

(Corridors are not the place for gossiping, club meetings or parties)

Auditorium Tips

During school years, a number of hours are spent in the school auditorium, listening to speeches or lectures, watching movies, or attending various programs. The auditorium requires the same good manners you would display in a public theater or lecture hall. At these places you wouldn't shove or push other people, talk in loud whispers, or pass notes if the performance or topic under discussion happened to bore you. If someone did these things to disturb you, you would probably become very upset, or in an indignant manner, ask the person to be quiet.

Sometimes a well-known person, a musician or scientist, gives his time to speak or perform in your assembly. This guest's impression of your school will be genuinely influenced by your conduct. By filing into the auditorium quickly and quietly, and giving your respectful attention will make the guest feel he or she is before an adult audience. Even if the subject or performance is uninteresting to you, whispering or passing notes is inexcusable. Picture yourself before a large group. How would you feel with a discourteous audience? The speaker or performer is probably an authority in his or her field. By being an attentive listener, you may get some new thoughts and ideas. At the end of the program a warm round of applause for the guest shows your appreciation and enjoyment.

Making Friends

Getting along with your schoolmates is an important part of school life. No matter how bright your teachers think you are, or how many times you make the honor roll, you probably won't feel happy or successful unless you have friends and feel you "belong" to some group. This is natural because people are social beings. They want to be liked and feel that they are a part of things.

Good manners are important in getting along with people. The considerate, thoughtful person is sure to be liked. Your consideration for others shows that you like them and want to please them. It is hard for anyone to resist this special and sincere attention.

There are some things about you that perhaps should not be important, but are. No matter how big your heart or wise your head, you are judged first by your appearance. People judge others that way. Haven't you seen someone new in your neighborhood or at school and decided on the spot that he or she was a good person? There was probably something about the person's looks and expressions—like a friendly smile—that made an instant good impression on you. First impressions are important and cannot be over estimated. The way you look and dress can either be a help, or a hindrance.

Edwardlene Fleeks Willis, Ph.D.

Personal Appearance

The basis for a good personal appearance for both boys and girls—men and women—is good health. There is no substitute for the right foods, lots of sleep, and outdoor exercise for bright eyes, clear skin, and shiny hair. Avoid skipping meals and ignoring curfews.

Even if you are a picture of good health, your friends may think of you as a bum if you fail to find time for careful grooming and dressing. Cleanliness is something you have heard parents or guardians talk about for as long as you can remember. There is no sense deciding which sweater or scarf goes best with what you are planning to wear until you have been through a daily routine bath (or shower), deodorant, toothbrush, hair brush, and clothes brush. After that you are ready for clean underwear, polished shoes, well-pressed skirt or pants, and a fresh blouse or shirt.

Girls usually have to allow five or ten minutes in their schedule before school to give their hair some extra brushing and to put on makeup skillfully. For school, a light dash of powder and lipstick are adequate.

School Clothes

Clothes for school don't have to be a problem. Girls often wear skirts and sweaters or simple tailored dresses and, more recently, jeans and slacks. Even if you must be at the height of fashion, avoid wearing sweaters or pants that are too baggy or too tight, and skirts that are either too long or too short. Learn which colors look well on you and stick to them.

Mind Your Manners
An Etiquette Guide for Youth and Young Adults

Being you is more important than following a fashion. Why try to look fashionable if the clothes are unbecoming to you? If you are definitely not the tailored type, wear a blouse with a collar under your sweater to give a little softness. Tie a small scarf around your neck if the color is right for you and your sweater. Whether you are a tweedy girl or a fluffy one, play it safe by always keeping your clothes simple and uncluttered. For boys, jeans or slacks with sport shirts and sweaters seem to be a school uniform. In some areas, shirts and ties and jackets are the custom. Follow the general trend in your school, but remember that it never hurts to be on the conservative side. Beware of tricky belts, loud colors, the too padded shoulders.

It is important to look at your entire wardrobe, consider its basic needs, and plan your buying at the beginning of the season. Decide on a wardrobe color scheme and before you go shopping know exactly what you want. Don't be tempted by every "marked down" or sale item. If it doesn't fit into your wardrobe plan, it's no bargain. Buy only the type of clothes suitable for your figure and the kind of life you lead. This routine should help you have a well-planned wardrobe instead of a closet full of ill-assorted clothes.

Edwardlene Fleeks Willis, Ph.D.

CHAPTER IV

PARTY MANNERS

A party can be anything from four people viewing a videocassette to a large formal affair. Most parties are an informal gathering of people at someone's home.

The main purpose of a party or dance is to have fun. This can be done if certain rules of etiquette are practiced.

Party Strategies

If you arrive at a party with an interest in whatever happens, and a desire to be friendly with everyone, chances are you are going to have a good time. A positive "party attitude" has a lot to do with making the party a success or failure. If you expect to have a good time, you probably will. If you are sure that it is going to be a flop and that no one will ask you to dance, the chances are good that that will happen.

For a party to be successful, everyone has to have a good time. This means no cliques or close groups, no pairing off and leaving the group, no critical or unkind talk, no neglecting one or two individuals. Everyone—including the hostess—has a responsibility in seeing that a party is a success, that no one feels "left out."

HINTS TO GIRLS: If you attend a no-date party, avoid the nearest group of females or staying close to your best friend. Make it easy for the boys. They may lack the bravery to crash a female group to ask you to dance. Go over to the group around the piano or the snack table and join in the conversation. Don't be afraid to approach a boy with a friendly remark. He may be looking for an opening too, so help him along.

For a successful party, let no one feel left out of the fun. When you go to friends' parties, treat their home with respect. Their parents have been kind in letting them have a party. Parents won't appreciate wet rings on the coffee table, or food stains on the rug. Such discoveries are likely to result in curtailing parties at your friends' homes.

Parents also dislike rough housing. Suddenly in the midst of the party a few of the fellows decide to practice football passes with the sofa pillow. This behavior starts harmlessly enough, but all too soon, chairs have been knocked over, tables kicked, and lamps broken. You can understand why parents disapprove of these activities.

(For a successful party, let no one feel left out of the fun.)

Edwardlene Fleeks Willis, Ph.D.

Formal Dances

The big spring formal is two months off, but everyone is already excited over it. Boys could save girls much unnecessary anguish if they would ask for a dale four to six weeks ahead of time. Call the lucky girl on the telephone and simply ask her for a date to the dance. There is no need to beat around the bush! If she already has a date for the dance she will tell you, or she will accept graciously without stalling while she pretends to think it over. If she accepts, discuss plans with her - what time you will call for her, transportation problems, if any; or any after-the dance plans. It may seem a bit early for this, but a date likes it better if details are taken care of before the last minute.

If you girls don't receive a bid for a dance, there is no need to be upset. It is perfectly proper to ask an escort, preferably an outsider, not a schoolmate - to the affair. Tell them that the dance is going to be formal. You are also responsible for arranging the transportation unless your date has a car at their disposal.

Formal Clothes

Ok, everyone has a date! Although boys have fewer preparations to make, they should get busy with them. If you are fortunate enough to own a tuxedo, be sure it is taken out of mothballs a week before the big night. Check the fit. Give it a good airing and brushing. Check on your clean dress shirt, black tie, shoes and socks. You will need two white handkerchiefs - one for show, and the other for your hip pocket. If you are to rent the tuxedo, do it early. Be sure it fits well. If this is your first formal, you should wear your new suit around the house for a few hours to get the feel - then you will be able to relax in it at the dance.

Mind Your Manners
An Etiquette Guide for Youth and Young Adults

Girls have more to do. Unless you are pretty lucky, you may have to wear one of your old formals, or perhaps one of your older sister's. This is no calamity. The success of the evening doesn't depend on a new dress. A dress that is really becoming and comfortable - in which you feel "right" - can help you glide into a room with real self-assurance. Avoid a dress that is so fussy that you have to concentrate on it rather than on your date. You have plenty of time for sequins and black satin. Most boys and men shy away from ultra-sophisticated clothes. Don't dress as if you have aged for the prom! Dress your age and be your most attractive self.

On the day of the formal affair, give yourself plenty of time for bathing and dressing. Give the whole effect, a careful once-over to be sure that you are at your best -and then forget about how you look. No hitching or hiking at clothes or fussing with hair once you are at the dance or some other formal - just have fun!

(Try out your formal clothes at home to feel more comfortable in them later.)

Edwardlene Fleeks Willis, Ph.D.

Corsages

It is customary in many communities for the boys to send his date a corsage if the dance is formal. The thoughtful date will call the girl a few days before the dance to ask what color the dress she is wearing. Since strapless dresses are popular, you might ask her if she prefers flowers to wear in her hair. Don't be afraid to ask the florist's advice. Maybe your date would like something besides the usual gardenia. If you are "in the money." an orchid corsage makes any girl feel extra special. The florist can deliver the flowers or you can bring them yourself when you call for your dale. Either is correct, but having the flowers delivered gives her time to put them on before you arrive.

Calling for Your Date

If nine o'clock is the time to pick up your date, please be prompt - neither early (she'll be flustered), nor late (she'll be anxious). If you are detained, be sure to telephone. The girl should make a special effort to be ready on time, too. After the boy arrives, it is not necessary to stay with the parents for long. Introduce your date, chat a bit, and tell them what time you expect to be home, and be off.

A boy may feel very gallant by now and, of course, helps his date in and out of the car, opens doors, takes her arm going up and down steps, and helps her off with her wrap. Greet the chaperone with a pleasant "Good evening". It takes very little time and effort and is the courteous thing to do.

Dance Cards

Dance cards or programs are often used at some affairs. Dances maybe listed by number and announced. Some are in honor of a special person or event. Filling out the dance card, if there is one, is the boy's job. He can monopolize his date for the evening if he chooses, but a little variety is probably more fun for both of you. He dances the first and last dances, and the ones before and after supper with his partner.

Subscription Dances/Stag Line

Dances given by a girl's school or a Sadie Hawkins dance at a public school are known as subscription dances. Girls may freely ask any boy to attend with them, and pay for their escorts tickets, as well as their own. The boys furnish transportation and corsages as appropriate, and entertainment, such as a snack after the dance.

If the dance is given at a boy's school, boys buy the tickets and provide local transportation to and from the dance. The girl or her parents properly pay for any major transportation costs (fare from a long distance).

Neither of you should be exhibitionists while dancing. Concentrate on your date and not on every other pretty girl or on the stag line. Incessant chatter is not necessary while you dance. Take your cue from each other. If a date wants to talk, keep the conversation light—then there will be no "chemistry" problems.

Boys on a stag line may cut in on a couple without an introduction, but once a girl has been cut in upon, she should remain with that new partner until the end of the dance.

(Boys and men should never leave a dance partner standing on the floor)

If you are on the stag line for a while and spot a girl you'd like to dance with seated on the sideline with her date, simply ask her, "Would you like to dance?" The boy always asks the girl, not her date. She can speak for herself. You never ask, "Is this dance taken?" A girl hates to admit that it isn't.

A direct and clear response from the girl like, "Yes, thank you, I'd like to" or "I'd love to" sounds better than "Uh, Huh", or "Who me?" When the number is over, the boy never leaves a girl on the dance floor, but always returns her to her date or a group of friends. A boy should never escort a girl or woman from the dance floor and leave her alone.

If a girl is dating an outsider, she should make a special effort to see that he is introduced to her crowd and that he has a good time.

If you need to repair your makeup during the dance, excuse yourself and do it in the powder room. Do not apply makeup in public.

Refusing a Dance

A girl or woman need not dance with anyone she doesn't care to. However, she should be polite in her refusal. She may say, "Thank you but I don't believe I'm free right now," if she is hoping for another partner. If she is tired, she should say, "Thank you, but I'd like to rest a little." If she really wants him to join her she may add, "Won't you join me?"

If the dance is too long and no relief seems in sight, either partner can suggest leaving the floor because it is crowded or get refreshments, talk or a walk outside might be more fun.

If either partner feels uncomfortable doing a particular dance and the band strikes up that tempo, this is another acceptable excuse for sitting out a dance.

After the dance a group may decide to go out together for some food. This is fine, but girls should remember to be considerate of their dates' finances. Most boys have a limited amount to spend—so girls don't order the most expensive thing on the menu.

The evening is over and has lived up to its promises. Be sure to tell your date what a wonderful evening it has been and what fun you have had.

Edwardlene Fleeks Willis, Ph.D.

CHAPTER V

ENTERTAINING

Since the 70's, entertaining is more relaxed and informal. It expresses the personal values and taste of the host and hostess rather than the rigid and formal social rules of the past. With this new wave of freedom, hosts are showing a passion for quality, whether in the choice of friends, foods, or furnishings that leads to natural ease and elegance.

Recognize that being allowed to entertain at home while still living with your parents is a privilege. You should remove anything that is fragile to avoid saying, "Please be careful!" Don't shoo the family out of sight the minute the guests arrive. Parents will probably be glad to go to a movie or somewhere else if they know in time, but it is courteous to introduce the guests to them first.

This can be done, in terms of entertaining, by being yourself, showing others your favorite things and your favorite people and creating your favorite atmosphere - whether casual, romantic, festive, exotic, nostalgic or dramatic—in comfortable surroundings.

To become an accomplished host and hostess, learn the basic technology of entertaining by taking classes in cooking and decorating; reading books, or watching shows, or entertaining; being a keen observer at various social affairs; or by consulting a professional. If you feel comfortable without professional help let your own natural gifts take over. Train yourself to be organized and plan parties in a thorough and efficient manner.

Mind Your Manners
An Etiquette Guide for Youth and Young Adults

Even the most relaxed hostess or host has shaky moments and experiences pre-party panic. Careful planning in advance will help things go smoothly. The ingredients of a successful party are congenial people, good music, a few well-timed and appropriate games, and plenty of food.

Invitations

Invite only as many guests as your room will hold comfortably. Be open about the invitations. Ask your friends at school or over the phone. You may send an informal little note of invitation. Mention the time you'd like everyone to be there, and the time the party ends. This will help avoid "breaking up" problems later on. Parties aren't usually planned for a school night, except Friday. Saturday night is usually best. Asking everyone to come alone avoids the pairing-up woes, but it is more pleasant if you can arrange to have each boy call for a girl and each man a woman!

Don't be too shy or afraid to invite a boy or girl who has never asked you for a date. Everyone is pleased to get invited to a party. Be sure to ask people in plenty of time before they make other plans.

Being a Good Host/Hostess

Greet guests at the door and guide them to the place where they can leave their wraps. Introduce those who don't know each other. There may be a lull until things get going, but don't worry. All parties usually go through a warming-up stage. Some quiet music or a pencil and paper game will start things going. If the boys group to one side of the room and the girls to the other, you might start dancing by having the boys turn their backs while each girl puts one shoe in the center of the room. Each boy then picks up a shoe and finds his "Cinderella", and there you are - ready for dancing.

A host or hostess should mingle with all the guests and not concentrate on any one person. Try to draw out any shy guest by giving him a job—taking care of the music, helping to serve refreshments. When there is a lull in activities, liven things up with a mixer or a game, but don't force the guests to do anything they don't feel like doing.

Refreshments

Food and drinks give a lift to any party. Prepare these ahead of time. They don't have to be elaborate, but should be plentiful and attractive. One easy favorite is to spread a table in another room with the fixings for sandwiches—all varieties of sliced breads and fillings. Add a few crisp greens, chips, dips plus soda, milk, chocolate syrup, ice cream for homemade sodas, and watch the crowd dig in. Serve the food around 10:30 so that there is time for a game or a few records before your party breaks up. You might ask a close friend to start the 'good nights', everyone will follow suit The boys should see to it that each girl is taken home, but the host/hostess must make sure that everyone is taken care of.

The mark of a really good hostess is to realize that you had fun at your own party: One job remains to be done—restoring the house to its original state.

Setting the Table

The correct way to set a table is something everyone should know. It is easy. Once you learn the few necessary rules. A word of advice: never crowd the table. If it is too small, turn your party into a buffet supper.

Keep the centerpiece low so that your guests can see each other. It can be fruit, flowers, or ornaments—keep it simple. Candles add a nice touch for special occasions.

Before setting the table, consider your menu—then you won't sit down to eat and realize you've forgotten spoons. Use a large tray to carry the china, glasses, and all silver on the table. It saves many steps and the tray can be used again when you clear the table.

Whether you decide to use mats or a tablecloth makes little difference, just so long as the linen is sparkling clean. All silverware on the table is brightly polished. Knives and spoons go to the right of the plate and forks to the left. Napkins, with the folded side toward the plate, go to the left of the forks. Pieces used first go on the outside, so that the diner works his way in toward the plate. All pieces of silver are placed an inch from the edge of the table, fork tines up, spoon bowls up, and the cutting edge of the knife toward the plate. The butter knife is placed across the rim of the butter plate, which is at the fork's tip. There is a service plate at every setting and a water glass at the tip of the knife. Salad plates go to the left of the forks, and cups and saucers at the right, next to the spoons.

Edwardlene Fleeks Willis, Ph.D.

(Setting a table correctly is easy once you learn the rules)

Table: 1. Napkin 2. Fish Fork 3. Salad Fork 4 Dinner Fork 5. Dinner Knife 6. Teaspoon 7. Soup Spoon 8. Cup and Saucer 9. Goblet 10. Dessert Fork 11. Dessert Spoon 12. Butter Knife and Butter Plate 13. Salad Plate **Note:** If table setting is confusing, watch your host/hostess. If you begin to use the wrong utensil, continue to use it for that course.

Check the table carefully before asking your guests to come in. Be sure you have the water, butter and rolls on, and all serving implements ready.

Table Manners

You may groan at the phrase, table manners, but the whole business is not really a nuisance. You eat at least three times a day. Some people have two sets of table manners— one for home and one for dining out, it is best to use good table manners every time you eat.

The safest rule to follow when you are faced with a strange array of eating implements is to work from the outside in. Keep your eye on the host or hostess, if there is one, and follow this lead.

When you are offered a platter of food, slip the serving spoon under a portion and hold it in place with a serving fork. Put it on your plate and return the serving utensils to the platter in their original positions. Take moderate portions. You can always come back for more. In a restaurant the waiter will usually relieve you of this concern. He will bring you food already on a plate or serve you himself.

When cutting one's food American-style, hold the fork in the left hand and the knife in the right hand. Then put down the knife and transfer the fork from the left to the right hand for putting food on the fork and into the mouth.

In the continental style, hold the fork in the left hand and the knife in the right for cutting purposes and for eating. Continue to hold the knife in the right hand and the fork stays in the left hand. There is no transfer of utensils. The knife also contains food, in a support role until it is safely on the fork.

Place the knife and fork side by side in the middle of your plate when you have finished eating.

When eating, never put salt and pepper on food before tasting it. If you are someone's guest, add salt and pepper sparingly and inconspicuously. Otherwise, your host will think the food was tasteless or poorly prepared. Never ask for steak sauce or catsup to go over a meal prepared by your host. It is an insult to the cook.

Edwardlene Fleeks Willis, Ph.D.

Never probe for food stuck in teeth with a toothpick or fingernails when you are at the table. If you are unable to dislodge it with your tongue, try to get through the meal until everyone is finished, and you can find a bathroom to take care of the situation. If the situation is unbearable, excuse yourself quickly from the table and make repairs in the bathroom. Vigorously rinsing your mouth with water often solves the problem.

Elbows on the table, while eating, make you look sloppy. They can be placed on the table between courses, if the hands are folded. An erect posture helps you eat more graciously and enjoy your food more. It also makes a good impression on your host.

There are a few rules to remember about napkins. Large dinner napkins are only half-unfolded; small luncheon napkins are spread out completely over the lap. Keep your napkin on your lap until you are ready to leave the table. Then fold it neatly and place it on the table as you leave it.

Often the question is asked, "How do you hold glasses?" A stemmed glassware or wineglass is held with the thumb and the first two fingers at the base of the bowl. If the glass contains a chilled drink, hold the glass by the stem. Hold a tumbler near its base.

A considerate host seats left-handed guest, whenever possible, so that they have a table end on their left side. This is also showing consideration for their right-handed tablemates seated next to them.

Mind Your Manners
An Etiquette Guide for Youth and Young Adults

Saying Grace

A guest should follow the customs of the house wherever he or she may be. If you are a guest at someone's home and no grace is said before the meals, do not say, "I think we ought to have grace (or give thanks)." It is better to say grace quietly by yourself. If you say grace in your home before meals, it is all right to say it with guests too. If they are already seated, do not make them stand, just say: "We will now say grace."

The rule is, to never leave an eating utensil in a bowl, compote, or cup. However, the exception to this rule is that after eating, if there is no room for your utensils on the under plate, you have no choice.

Everyone eats chicken quite properly with his or her fingers at a picnic or barbecue. If you are a guest in someone's home, use a knife and fork until you are unable to cut off any more. If your hosts pick up their pieces of chicken "at the end" to get at those last hard-to-reach morsels on the bone, you may do likewise.

Do not pick up your chicken if you are served roast or fried chicken at a formal dinner. Chicken cooked in a casserole dish is never picked up.

Bacon is eaten with your fingers only if it is crisp and not covered with grease or a sauce.

Take one kind of food on your plate at a time. It is permissible to cut several mouth-size bites of food at a time, but do not cut the entire piece of meat or all the food on the plate. When the knife is not being used, place it along the top of the plate, the cut edge toward you. Do not talk with your mouth full or make any unnecessary noise. Sometimes the crunch of crisp celery cannot be helped, but the slurping of soup or coffee is carelessness and bad manners. To determine whether some food can be eaten with the fingers, watch your host/hostess. If you are eating at a restaurant, use your common sense. Food like fried chicken can be picked up as well as cut up.

Check yourself on table manners:

		YES	NO
1.	Do you sit at the table without playing with the silverware?	___	___
2.	Do you wait until every one has been served or your hostess has begun before you start eating?	___	___
3.	Do you try any new food served you without picking at it suspiciously?	___	___
4.	Do you take a forkful of food at a time without mixing everything together on your plate?	___	___
5.	Do you place your knife and fork neatly across the rim of your plate and not in scattered directions when you finish eating?	___	___

Answers to all of the questions should be "yes". If not, practice up on your manners beginning at the family table, so the next time you are dining out, you will feel confident about doing the right thing.

Buffet Supper

This form of entertaining has become increasingly popular because of its informality and convenience for the host and or hostess.

A buffet supper is an easy way of handling a large crowd. You can design the table any way you wish. One way is to push the table against the wall and have a tall dramatic centerpiece at the back of the table. The main idea is to make self-service easy, and to have everything within reach. Carve the meat. Butter the rolls. The plates, napkins, and silver should all be at one of the tables so that people know where to start. Put your main dishes in the center and keep the vegetables and relishes nearby. Accolades will come to you from your family and friends when you treat them to a buffet of great dishes that are tasteful and appealing.

Equipment and Supplies

Young adults often seek advice on what basic items are needed for entertaining. These include electrical equipment, equipment for the table and table accessories. The following selections were made with different budgets in mind:

1. Electrical Equipment

Basic
Blender
Mixer
Electric coffee maker
Toaster

Economical
Toaster oven
Microwave oven
Deep fat fryer/cooker
Electric skillet
Hot tray
Wok

Luxury
Food processor
Mixer with accessories
Ice Crusher
Ice Maker
Hot Table
Espresso machine

2. Table Equipment

Basic
Linen: 6 place mats of machine washable fabric, straw or plastic
6 napkins of machine washable fabric

Economical
Solid or print tablecloths
Matching or contrasting napkins
Heatproof place mat pads
Fine fabric or linen place mats
Mirror place mats

Luxury
Embroidered linens
Lace or appliqued cloths
Accessorized napkins
Colored linen cloths

a: China

Basic
White iron stone service for 8, including 8 dinner plates, 8 cups and saucers, 8 salad, bread-and-butter dishes, one serving bowl, 2 platters

Economical
China or earthenware service for 12, including dinner plates, salad bowls, fruit plates, one 14-inch platter, one 16 inch platter, 2 vegetable service dishes

Luxury
5-piece china service for 24, 24 cream soups and saucers, 24 demitasse cups and saucers (maxed or mixed), 2-16 inch platters, 1 oversized platter for turkey, poached fish, etc., 3 large serving bowls, 24 fruit saucers, 1 gravy bowl, 24 artichoke plates, Large covered tureen Cake and pedestal dishes covered tureen Cake and pedestal dishes

b. Flatware

Basic
Stainless flatware service for 8

Economical
Silver plate, 5-piece settings, service for 12 plus:
12 teaspoons
12 butter spreaders
2 serving spoons
2 serving forks
1 cold meat fork
1 cake server
1 gravy ladle
1 sugar spoon
1 soup ladle
1 carving knife and fork
1 salad serving spoon and fork

Luxury
Sterling silver 6-piece setting, service for 12 or 24
1 sterling tea and coffee service with tray
12 additional spoons
12 or 24 cocktail forks
12 or 24 fruit knives and forks
12 or 24 cream soups
12 or 24 fish forks
12 or 24 fish knives
12 or 24 stemmed sherbets
3 cold meat forks
2 gravy ladles
1 soup ladle
2 or 4 tablespoons
1 or 2 salad serving forks
1 or 2 salad serving spoons
1 carving fork and knife
1 long handled stuffing spoon
1 cake server
1 cheese server

c. Glassware

Basic
8 goblets, eight 8-ounce wines
8 old-fashioned glasses

Economical
12 goblets, 12 wines, 12 champagnes
12 cordials, 12 highballs, 12 double old-fashioneds
12 snifters 12 pilsners, 12 finger bowls

Luxury
24 goblets
24 tulip wine glasses

24 balloon wine glasses
24 champagne glasses
24 snifters
24 cordials
24 highballs
24 old-fashioned
24 crystal salad or service plates
finger bowls

3. Table Accessories

Basic
Salad bowl, pitcher, wine flask
2 to 4 candle holders
flower vase
coffee and/or tea pot

The amount a person spends on additional table accessories depends on the materials from which they are made, as well as the quantity in which one buys them. Sterling silver accessories, for example, represent a greater financial investment than glass or pewter. With this in mind, the following accessories might be added to your basic entertainment equipment: pitchers, decanters, coolers, lidded or plain serving dishes, tureens, relish dishes, fruit and flower bowls (regular sized), bud vases, candle-sticks, a candelabra, and food warmers. Other purely decorative objects can take any form, according to personal taste and imagination.

Having fun at Parties

Going out to parties and dances and entertaining at home can be wonderful fun. According to the law of averages, you are going to have some bad times as well as some good times. But with the aid of organization and planning, good manners,

Edwardlene Fleeks Willis, Ph.D.

and a cheery, positive attitude, you can make the good times come out on top.

CHAPTER VI

DATING ETIQUETTE

When most teenagers think of popularity, they think in terms of the opposite sex. This is natural and understandable. Usually a great deal of time is spent thinking about ways in which to pursue the matter further. If you avoid getting too intense about it all you will have more peace of mind. By not assuming a do-or-die attitude, you will develop smoother relationships with the others; you don't have to be a terrific hit on every date.

As you look around you will see that there are quite a number of the opposite sex. Do you think you can or want to captivate all of them? Aren't you being over optimistic to consider every fellow or girl as the Big Romance? You can have a good time together with the opposite sex just being friends—taking a walk, talking, playing tennis or listening to recordings. By taking it easy and knowing some of the rules of dating etiquette, you will find the faster route toward your goal to become more confident and popular.

Getting a Date

The male is the luckier one in this situation because all he usually has to do is ask for a date. Occasionally the girls turn him down, but generally boys do have the edge. They can pick and choose. The initiative is up to them. They don't usually ever have to be dateless if they don't want to be.

How about a female? What can she do about this dating situation? There are several possibilities. She can ask one of her close friends to arrange a double date. She can plan an informal party and ask any boy in school. But the best way to get dates is to be friendly but not over friendly, in all school and social contacts; to join in school projects and extra-curricular activities; and to participate in young people's community activities. These suggestions are not a hundred percent guaranteed, but they work surprisingly well.

(Knowing dating do's and don'ts help your popularity dreams come true.)

Accepting a Date

If a fellow stops a girl in the hall at school to ask for a movie date on Friday night, she should answer with a prompt "Thanks, (fellow's name), it sounds like fun," if she wants to go. If she would rather not, a simple "no, thanks, (fellow's name), I can't make it" will do for an answer. Elaborate excuses aren't necessary, but the excuse should be fair. If a fellow spots the girl out with another fellow on the night she said was reserved for washing her hair, it will be a long time before he calls her again. This news will also spread to other potential dates.

It is also bad practice for a girl to break a date unless she has to—never because someone she prefers has asked her later. This will soon put a girl on a fellow's blacklist. Too, it is a discourteous thing to do. Even a second-choice fellow has feelings that should be respected. A girl would not like it if a fellow called her just before their date to say he had to baby-sit for his parents, and later she discovered that he was out with another girl. Don't ignore someone else's feelings to satisfy a selfish whim.

Dressing for a Date

It is up to the fellow to let the girl know what sort of date he is planning. Is it to be a walk, a movie, bowling, party, dancing? This will give her a cue about how to dress. Grooming and dressing for a dale are similar as for any other occasion, except that extra care is indicated. Cleanliness is basic. Give extra attention to secure buttons and snaps and straight stockings for girls; pressed trousers and clean shirts for fellows, and brushed hair and straight heels for both.

(Tell your date the plans for the evening so she will know how to dress.)

Attending certain events with an escort gives a girl an opportunity to dress with variety and individuality. This doesn't mean over-fussy clothes or extreme styles. A skirt or slacks with a soft blouse or a simple dress is fine for a movie. Wear your best daytime dress to a party, but wear your best after-five dress or formal to the dance.

When fellows come calling for their date, show by your clothes what sort of occasion it is to be. Dress according to the affair. A girl who is dressed for a party feels uncomfortable if her date arrives dressed for bowling. A fellow should have one suit in his wardrobe for necessary occasions. This could be a gray or blue mens-wear material or a Glen plaid or a tweed, depending on your preference.

Having a Good Date

The following is a list of questions to help you determine if you are a good date. Some of the questions apply to both sexes. Read both lists, and check each answer "yes" or "no".

Females

		YES	NO
1.	Do you fidget with your clothes?	___	___
2.	Do you make critical remarks about yourself as a come-on for compliments?	___	___
3.	Do you smile only when amused?	___	___
4.	Is your evening spoiled if someone accidentally spills something on your dress?	___	___
5.	Are you preoccupied with your appearance?	___	___
6.	Do you get upset if you have to play a game that you feel makes you look silly?	___	___
7.	If you're having conversation troubles do you give up in despair?	___	___
8.	Do you sulk if you think the party is a flop?	___	___
9.	Do you overdo being "hard-to-get"?	___	___

10. Do you give detailed reports?

Males

1. Do you sit back and wait to be amused?
2. Do you abandon your date to talk to a group at another table?,
3. Do you show her photos of previous dates?
4. When you're in a group, do you get attention by talking louder than anyone else?
5. Do you embarrass your date by talking loudly in public?
6. Do you overdo your sociability with practical jokes?
7. Do you chew your fingernails?
9. Do you scorn chivalry, such as helping her in and out of cars and holding doors open?
10. Do you talk only about sports instead of discussing her interests part of the time?
11. Do you ignore the curfew set by her parents?

If you answered "no" to all of these questions, your dating etiquette excellent. If you checked "yes" to one or more questions, you need to brush up on your manners.

A date is a fifty-fifty proposition. It will never succeed with a bored, "now make-me-enjoy-it" attitude. It takes work. You have to make a sincere effort in time and energy to be friendly and genuinely interested in people.

Good looks are an asset, but they are not the whole story. There should be something behind those beautiful eyes, or handsome face to attract the opposite sex. Know what is going on in your school, your community, and the world. An interesting person is a better date. Be pleasant, fair, honest, and maybe a little unpredictable, but be yourself.

Conversing with Others

No one can put the right words in your mouth or give a secret formula for witty talk. However, there are things you can do to cover up those embarrassing periods of silence that often occur in conversation with the other sex. Common sense, basic intelligence, interest in other people, and a sense of humor make a good conversationalist.

(Discovering someone's interests and having some of your own give you something to talk about)

When girls are together, they can talk endlessly about clothes and dates; and boys have a whole world, of sports to discuss. When it comes to talking to each other, both sexes shut up like clams. A fellow sees a pretty girl at a party, and for the life of him can't think of a clever opening remark.

Why must it be clever? Why not an easy, "My name is Miles Stevens. I was wondering if you would like to dance."

If a boy is tense and over anxious about the impression he is going to make, he won't think of the girl at all. Try to shift your thoughts to the other person. Acquire a genuinely friendly interest in the thoughts and feelings of others. If you can practice and accomplish this, you won't have time to worry about yourself. You can't fake a good conversation. Picking a topic at random and not caring what sort of a response you will get doesn't work.

When you are trying to find a person's interests, don't do it by asking questions in rapid-fire order. If you are enthusiastic about a topic, chances are your enthusiasm will be contagious and you will both be chatting easily before you know it. There is more to a good conversation than to ask questions. You should have some definite opinions and ideas yourself. This makes for better conversation and helps sell your ideas. It makes you a more interesting person.

Things to avoid in a conversation

1. Don't cut off a conversation with a negative answer. Try to keep the conversation going.
2. Don't interrupt with dozens of questions; wait until the person is through talking.
3. Don't raise your voice unpleasantly.
4. Don't let a conversation die, even if you are stuck with the dullest person in the room.
5. Don't make exaggerated gestures when you are telling a story.
6. Don't always quote others. Form your own opinions.
7. Don't develop a "line"—You may catch yourself on it.

Edwardlene Fleeks Willis, Ph.D.

Tricky conversation situations:

A little common sense will help you through most of them.

1. If you meet a fellow's ex-girl, stay clear of the sore spot and don't talk about the fellow.
2. If you're with two people you know but who don't know each other, talk about things all three of you have in common.
3. If you bump into your best friend's girl, talk to her as you would any other girl. She is not in a special category.
4. If you meet an ex-date's mom or dad on the streets, don't duck out of sight. Say "Hello, Mr./Mrs./Ms. So-and-So," and let them take it from there.
5. If you meet and ex-boyfriend when you're with another fellow, be casual and talk about the weather or other general things.

Having Blind Dates

There is a never-ending argument about the value of blind dates. Some people believe it is an invitation for a dull evening with the world's biggest jerk. Others believe you can meet some nice people that way. This is something you have to decide. There are some unwritten rules on the making of blind dales. If the date is arranged by a mutual friend, and if there will be other people along, it is in perfectly good taste to ask or accept. But dates with strangers, or single-dates, are definitely not a good idea.

The success of a blind date depends mainly on your attitude. It can be dull and dismal or an exciting adventure.

Mind Your Manners
An Etiquette Guide for Youth and Young Adults

The trouble is that people usually dream of all sorts of wonderful qualities for their unknown partner. When the person turns out to be just another date, they are disappointed; and too often show their disappointment.

If you have a good time on your blind date, that's great! Don't start out expecting him or her to be out of this world. Chances are this won't be the case. Even if you are not overly impressed, you can still have fun if you try. It is unpardonable to be sulky and spoil the evening for everyone else.

Restaurant Rules

A dinner date is a special occasion. The waiter will show you a table. The girl or woman follows the waiter with the fellow following. If a waiter is not available, the fellow does the honors—he helps the girl or woman off with her coat and holds the chair for her.

Complicated menus can be bewildering, but take your time. If the waiter comes right over for your order, you can always tell him you are not quite ready. Menus printed in foreign languages can be particularly puzzling. The waiter will be glad to explain what a particular dish is, if you ask him. However, there are a few common French phrases you should know. **Table d'hote** means that you get a complete meal for the price of the main dish, or **entree**, as it is called. **A la Carte** means that each dish is priced separately. This plan is more expensive than **table d' hote**.

Hors d'oeuvres, or appetizers—fruit juice, seafood cocktails, or crackers/ biscuits topped with caviar, anchovies, or similar delicacies—are served first. At the end of the meal you might have a **parfait**—several flavors of ice cream in a tall, thin glass with a spot of whipped cream on top. The girl tells her date what she will have and he gives both orders to the waiter.

At the end of the meal the girl can excuse herself to touch up her makeup in private. A girl's purse should be in her lap, not on the table. Her date rises when she gets up and also when she returns to the table. He also stands if anyone (male or female) should stop at the table to chat. When he gets the check from the waiter, it is perfectly proper to look it over and add up the total. Tipping varies from place to place, but never leave less than ten percent; fifteen is probably better. It is poor taste to over tip as to under tip. The fellow should have enough money with him so he doesn't have to borrow from his date.

Going Steady

Going steady gives a wonderful, secure feeling—a sense of belonging that we all like. The majority of teenagers are not ready for a permanent attachment. If you and your steady date understand that your relationship is just a temporary thing, you will not get involved in something more serious than you bargained for.

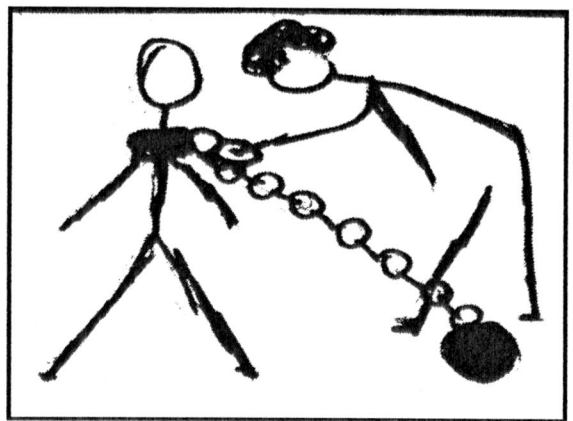

(Boys usually shy away from girls who have that "you-belong-to-me" attitude.)

Girls tend to build up a relationship too much on being asked out two or three times by the same fellow. They would be wiser to skip that "you-belong-to me" attitude. Boys usually shy away from possessive girls.

Frequently couples continue to go steady simply because it's the easiest thing to do: They've fallen into the habit and are lazy about making new friends. As a general rule, you will get the more fun and benefit from keeping a large social circle. One of the values of dating is that it gives you a chance to find out what kind of person you will want some day to marry. By dating many kinds of people you will be able to make a better choice when that important day comes.

Breaking Up

Suppose two people have been going together steadily for several months, and one of them wants to end the relationship. Unfortunately, it is seldom a mutual feeling.

That would make breaking up fairly simple. The girl may have a crush on the new boy in the neighborhood, or a fellow may feel that the girl is getting too serious about their relationship. It may be that the two of you just haven't as much in common as you thought.

There are several ways of breaking up a friendship that involve unpleasantness and injured feelings. Standing up your steady on an important date would end things quickly, but with the least tact and courtesy. You both may have found yourselves quarreling more frequently. So you have one big fight that results in really hurt feelings. This type of breakup is not a satisfactory solution.

A gradual parting of the ways is best. A fellow might call the girl less frequently or walk her home from school less regularly. A weekend night might go by—and no date. It could happen quite gradually without too much pain. A girl would have to refuse some dates and generally not be so available. When the fellow sees her with someone new and then, he'll catch on. In the meantime, he has had time to mend his pride and date another girl. The main point is to try to spare the other person from having hurt feelings, to part peacefully and remain friends.

Ending a Date

There is a lot of confusion about ending a date. Boys claim that the girls want to be kissed goodnight, and the girls say the boys expect to be kissed. Who is right?

As with many aspects of boy-girl relations, the girl is the one who makes the decisions, who controls the situation. This may seem unfair, but that's the way it is. If a girl decides she doesn't want to be kissed goodnight, then she can simply act

Mind Your Manners
An Etiquette Guide for Youth and Young Adults

in a way that will tell the boy how she feels. Take that pause at the door, for example. Before the moment of silence has had a chance to grow into anything, she can simply give her hand to the boy, smile, and say how much she has enjoyed herself. This is followed by a firm "Good night." And the opening of the door. The boy will take his cue from the girl. It is only the occasional fellow who will persist after the girl discourages him.

Then there's the question of when to kiss a date goodnight. The answer, to some extent, depends on the community in which you live, and the customs of your crowd. In some groups it is considered poor taste to kiss every casual date, although it is perfectly all right to kiss a fellow or girl you have dated for some time. In other groups a goodnight kiss is not taken quite so seriously. However, it is still a personal matter, and you should not feel you have to do what others do. When in doubt, don't! It is possible to err on the side of too many kisses, but you're usually safe in being choosy about the matter. Most fellows or girls won't be offended if you tactfully get out of the situation.

Another question that often bothers girls is whether to ask the boy in when they get home from a date. If it is fairly early and your parents are up, it's perfectly all right to ask the fellow in for a soft drink and sandwiches. But stay away from possible involvement of late hours and a dark or empty house.

CHAPTER VII

HOW TO BEHAVE IN PUBLIC

Etiquette touches every part of life. It is practiced at home, in school, on the job, and in social relations. For some situations there are special sets of rules. But there are many general tips that will be used in many places, many times, all your life. It is important to learn how to behave in public as soon as you can!

At the Movies

While dating, you will probably attend many movies. You should know how to behave well there, too!

When a fellow asks a girl or woman for a movie date, he should consult her about the feature she would like to see. She is his guest and he should try to please her. If he has his heart set on a war movie and she wants to see the latest musical, the musical it should be.

Some theaters have ushers who will show you to a seat. The fellow follows the girl, who follows the usher down the aisle. If there is no usher, the fellow will lead the way and find the seats. If two couples are together, they can either alternate boy, girl, boy, girl—or the girls can sit together in the center. Once you are seated, watch the show, don't put one on! Talking, giggling and rattling candy papers are extremely annoying to the rest of the audience.

Mind Your Manners
An Etiquette Guide for Youth and Young Adults

Attending a performance

You can show good manners when you go to a performance by doing these things:

1. Bring only things that are absolutely necessary (like a small purse or wallet), so that you will not take up unnecessary space in and around your seat.
2. Be on time for the performance so that you will not cause a disturbance by being late.
3. Let the people who were at the preceding performance out of the theater before you go in. Wait your turn patiently. Do not crowd or push your way into the theater.
4. Have your money or ticket ready so that you will not cause people behind you to wait.
5. Go to the restroom or get refreshments before you sit down and during intermission so that you will not have to get up during the performance.

(Once you're seated in a theater, watch the movie or performance; don't put on one of your own!)

Arriving After a Performance Begins

1. Wait for the usher to seat you if you arrive after performance has begun.

2. If there is no usher to seat you, wait for your eyes to adjust to the dark and then quickly and quietly find your seat.
3. If you have been assigned a seat, sit in it without complaining.
4. If you must pass in front of others to get to your seat, face the stage or screen when you are passing them. Try not to bump people or step on their toes.
5. Do not say anything unless you accidentally bump into someone or step on someone's toes. If you do this, say, "Excuse me" very softly.

Watching a Performance

1. Do not bother anyone around you by whispering, talking loudly, or doing other rude things like humming, whistling, snapping or popping gum, or tapping or kicking the seats in front of you.
2. If eating during the performance is permitted, do so neatly and quietly.
3. If someone needs to pass in front of you to get to a seat, pull your legs in or stand up so that the person can get by easily. If the person says, "Excuse me," you may want to say, "Surely."
4. If you find that you do not like a live performance, do your best to wait it out until intermission or the end of the performance. Try not to leave in the middle.
5. Avoid criticizing the performance while it is taking place. Wait for intermission, or preferably until after you leave the theater.
6. You should show appreciation for the performance by applauding at the appropriate times.
7. Do not begin to put your things on or to leave the theater before the performance is over.

8. When you leave, do not leave any trash or litter behind you. Always clean up after yourself.

Attending Athletic Events

Many of the rules that apply to the theater also apply to athletic events. When you attend an athletic event, you should show the same courtesy and sensitivity you would show at a theater performance.

Visiting a Church

In regard to another person's religion, you can be courteous by doing these things:

1. Never criticize or make fun of another person's religion.
2. Ask questions about a person's religion only if you are genuinely interested.
3. Before you visit a church, find out ahead of time whether there is any special way you should dress, and then dress accordingly. For example, some churches will require that you cover your head and/or arms.
4. Find out ahead of time what is going to take place during the service so that you will know when you should and should not participate. For example, some churches will offer communion to their members, while in other churches it doesn't matter.
5. It is not necessary for you to do everything the church members are doing, but you may feel more comfortable if you stand when they stand, sit when they sit, or kneel when they kneel.

6. During the service, it is extremely important that you be respectful. Sit quietly and pay attention as much as possible to what is going on.

Going Shopping

When shopping, you can be gracious by doing these things:

1. When a salesperson says, "May I help you?" answer. "Yes, please" (if you want help), or "No, thank you, I would prefer to look for a while", (if you do not want help).
2. Do not interrupt a salesperson that is helping another customer. Wait your turn to be helped.
3. Do not complain to sales people about prices. They have nothing to do with them.
4. Do not handle merchandise you do not intend to buy.
5. Handle all merchandise carefully.
6. If you break or damage something, call it to a salesperson's attention and offer to pay for it.
7. If you try on clothes, put them back on hangers after you have finished. Do not leave them on the dressing room floor.
8. Do not use anything you plan to return, and return it as soon as possible.

Riding in a Vehicle

You can show good manners whenever you board a car, bus, train or airplane by doing these things:

1. Be on time for departure so that you will not keep anyone waiting.

Mind Your Manners
An Etiquette Guide for Youth and Young Adults

2. Let the people who are already in the vehicle get out before you get in.
3. Do not crowd or push your way in the vehicle. Wait your turn patiently.
4. Have your money or ticket ready so that you won't cause people behind you to wait.
5. If you have been assigned a seat, sit in it without complaining.
6. If you have not been assigned a seat sit in the first available one.
7. If you have baggage or packages, keep them under your seat or in your lap. Do not take up additional space with them.
8. If someone else needs your seat more than you do, be kind and give it up. If you must stand, hold onto something so that you will not fall or bump into anyone.
9. Do not bother anyone around you by talking too loudly.
10. Do not do other rude things like reading over a person's shoulder.
11. Do not expect the person sitting next to you to entertain you. Converse with the person only if talk is encouraged.
12. Do not leave trash or litter behind when you leave.
13. If you are in an inside seat, excuse yourself when you are ready to leave, and avoid bumping into others or stepping on toes.
14. Excuse yourself if you need to make way through a crowd to the door, and avoid bumping into people or stepping on their feet as you go.
15. Leave the vehicle as soon as possible after it has come to a complete stop so that you will not detain the passengers who wish to board.

16. Take something along to entertain yourself while riding in a vehicle, like a deck of cards, a game, or some puzzles. Take pencils and paper for drawing or writing; take a book or magazine to read. Take something along to listen to like a cassette recorder or radio. (Do this only if your radio or recorder has headphones, so that you won't impose what you are listening to on the passengers around you.)

Riding an Elevator

1. Give the people who an leaving the elevator a chance to get out before you get in.
2. If an elevator is crowded wait for it to come back to you or take another one instead of squeezing your way in.
3. Push the button for the floor you want as you enter the elevator unless there is an elevator attendant to do it for you: If you can't get near the button, kindly ask someone standing near the button to push it for you.
4. Step to the back of the elevator if there are several stops ahead of you, so you will not stand in the way of people needing to get out before you.
5. Stay to the front of the elevator, but step to one side, if possible, if you will be getting off the elevator soon, so that you will not have to push through everyone to get out.

Mind Your Manners
An Etiquette Guide for Youth and Young Adults

    6. Say "Excuse me, may I get out?" or "Out, please," instead of pushing and shoving your way out of an elevator, so people in front of you can move out of your way.

Riding an Escalator

1. Wait your turn to get on the escalator or moving ramp.
2. Allow a few spaces to pass before you step on so you do not stand too close to the person who has stepped onto the escalator right before you.
3. Stand to your far right so that people may pass you on your left, if you are not in a hurry and want to stand still on the escalator. Make sure you do not block someone who wants to pass you.
4. Carefully pass the person in front of you on the left side and say, "Excuse me" as you pass if you are in a hurry and want to walk on the escalator.

Here are some questions to check your public demeanor:

		YES	NO
1.	Do you have your fare ready when you board a vehicle?	___	___
2.	Do you let swinging doors bang into people behind you?	___	___
3.	Do you talk loudly on a bus or a crowded elevator?	___	___
4.	Are you pleasant to bus drivers?	___	___
5.	Do you respect the privacy of a celebrity and refrain from mobbing him/her for an autograph?	___	___
6.	Do you wait until people get off a vehicle or elevator before you get in?	___	___
7.	Do you comb your hair or put on makeup		

	in public?	___	___
8.	Are you courteous to salespeople?	___	___
9.	Do you finish your breakfast at home, rather than on the bus?	___	___
10.	Do you chew gum violently in public?	___	___

For a perfect score you should have answered "yes" to questions 1, 4, 5, 6, 8 and 9, and "no" to 2, 3, 7, and 10.

Good Manners with Your Gang

For some reason, a perfectly civilized, courteous individual is often changed into a barbarian when with a gang in public. Passengers on buses and streetcars are often annoyed by noisy groups of teenagers, shrieking and playing around, and generally taking over the whole vehicle. Pedestrians often have to get out of the way when a gang sweeps down the street, taking possession of the entire sidewalk.

Teenagers have, in many instances, the urge to "take over" when they are in groups. This includes the corner diner, a record store, or other places where they hang out. It's sometimes difficult for a customer to even get in the door of these places! Each teenager, individually, may be thoughtful, sweet, and quiet. In order for the public to know this, try to have some consideration for others when you are with the gang.

Smoking, Alcohol and Drugs

Youth is a time of experimentation and to some the forbidden has a special appeal. Many young people decide to smoke or try alcohol or drugs because they see adults using them at home, restaurants, on television, etc. Young people

Mind Your Manners
An Etiquette Guide for Youth and Young Adults

frequently imitate adults. Often the opinion of peers, friends and gang members, has a great influence on them to smoke or use drugs. The pressure to try drugs is widespread. Sometimes it is hard to resist the rest of the group. Too, many boys and girls are curious about the effects of smoking. They may also experiment with alcohol and drugs and decide to try them to find out how it feels to get "high".

You will not lose friends if you refuse to try smoking, alcohol and drugs because those who want you to try these things are not your friends. Turn them down! The right choice, the right response is a quick but firm and courteous NO!

Problems related to smoking, drugs and alcohol could be avoided if you understand how they affect your mind and body.

The problem is that we do not always or even sometimes know these things. Knowing how to identify drugs by their trade names and slang term, their symptoms, as well as other related problems can help in the decline of experimenting with illegal substances.

They are especially dangerous for you because of the following:

- ❖ Smoking and drugs are harmful to your health;
- ❖ It is illegal to buy alcohol or cigarettes unless you are of legal age;
- ❖ Distribution or possession of drugs without a prescription is illegal.

Some examples of drugs that are commonly abused include:

Edwardlene Fleeks Willis, Ph.D.

Stimulants

Cocaine (snow, flake, gold dust)
Amphetamines (pep pills, speed, bennies, dexies, uppers), dextroamphetamine and methamphetamine (speed, diet and pep pills).

Depressnnts

Benzodiazepines (downers, goof balls, sleeping pills, candy)
<u>Chemical names:</u> Ativan, Azene, Clonopin, Diazepam, Dalmane, Librium, Xanax, Serax, Valium, Tranxene, Vestran, Versed, Halcion, Paxipam, Restoril
Glutethimide (Doriden)
Methaqualone (lude, quay, quad, mandrex)
<u>Chemical name:</u> Quaalude
Barbiturates (uppers, yellow jackets, red devils, phennies, barbs often named for color of pill)
<u>Chemical names:</u> Phenobarbital, pentobarbital, secobarbital, amobarbital
Others: Tranquilizer (Muscle relaxants, sleeping pills)

Narcotics

Opium
Heroin (horse, "H", junk, smack, dope, hard stuff)
Codeine (schoolboy)
Morphine ("M", morphic, hocus, white stuff)
Methadone (dollies, dolls) Amidane (a synthetic);
Darvon, Talrvin
Paregoric
Meperidine

Other Slang terms: T's and Blues, Designer drugs, China white

Cannabis

Tetrahdrocannabinol (THC)
Marijuana (pot, grass, weed, reefer, roach),
Names: Chronic, Acapulco Gold, Sinsemilla, Thai Sticks
THC, Hashish (hash) Hashish Oil (hash oil)
<u>Chemical Name:</u> Marinol

Organic Solvents

Inhalants (sniffing, glue sniffing, huffing)
Names: Gasoline, airplane glue, vegetable spray, hair spray, deodorants, spray paint, liquid paper, paint thinner, window cleaner, automobile products: freon, brake and transmission fluid, steering fluid, de-icers, auto body cleaners, car engine cleaners, octane boosters.

Hallucinogens

LSD(acid, microdoi, cubes)
Names: Lysergic acid, diethylamide, Mescaline and Peyote (Mese buttons, cactus)
Amphetamine variants (Ecstasy, designer drugs)
Names: 2, 5DMA, PMA, SMP, MDA, MDMA, TMA, DOM, DOE Phentyclidine (pop, angel dust, hog, peach pill)

Steroids

Danabol, Anavar, Android, Winstrol, Oreton, and Nilevar

Edwardlene Fleeks Willis, Ph.D.

Some symptoms of abuse from using stimulants are: loss of appetite, excitability and hyperactive body movement, excessive talking, trembling hands, enlarged pupils, heavy perspiration, compulsive behavior, dryness of mucus membranes, and lack of sleep.

Symptoms of abuse from using depressants include: drowsiness or lethargy, slurred speech and slowed body movements, drifting off in a trance, unsteady walk, quick temper, faulty judgment and depression.

Alcohol and drugs can interfere with your growth; add to stress, slow you down; change your mood; cause you to lose your self-respect and the respect of others; lead to reckless behavior; and make you do things you will regret.

The short-term effects of alcohol and drug usage are fairly easy to document and they are tragic enough. What may be even more pathetic are the long-term consequences involving addiction or disease, destruction and even crimes that are attributable to what begins as experimentation or a desire to get "high". This may end in poverty and misery not only on oneself, but on innocent unborn victims. Talk honestly with your family members, friends, teachers, and counselors about how smoking, alcohol and drugs can affect people. If you know someone who has a drug abuse problem, urge him or her to get help. You are responsible for your own destruction or triumph! Think for yourself. Don't go along with what everyone else is doing if you know it is wrong or harmful.

CHAPTER VIII

GENERAL TIPS ON ETIQUETTE

Introductions

You will always make introductions, either at home or in public. It will save you a good deal of embarrassment if you know how to do it properly. Using a little common sense will tell you when an introduction is more of a nuisance than a courtesy. In a crowded elevator or rows apart in a theater, for example, introductions are not necessary. However, on many occasions you will be called to perform the honors.

Always speak names clearly and use the first and last names of young people and adults. Each of the following phrases is appropriate:

> May I present Bob Jones? (This is somewhat formal)
> May I introduce Jean Murray?
> I would like for you to meet Virginia Green.
> This is Tom parks.

Introductions work out something like this: "Mary, this is Bob Jones; Bob, Mary Johnson." Or: "Mother, I'd like you to meet Mary Johnson and Bob Jones; Mary and Bob, this is my mother." Or if you are introducing your father and the principal of your school: Mr. Flynn, may I present my father, Mr. Walker; Dad, this is Mr. Flynn."

There are rules about who gets introduced to whom. Generally men are presented to women regardless of age, and young men and young women are presented to older men and older women, respectively. In a big crowd, get everyone's attention and then go around in a circle. In a large group you may not have been introduced to everyone. Then it is perfectly all right to introduce yourself. It is all right to ask that a name be repeated if you did not hear it the first time. If you are trying to put strangers at ease with each other, start the conversation rolling for them. Mention some interest they might have in common or an outstanding achievement of one of them.

When two men or boys meet they almost always shake hands. Two women or girls can do so if they wish. When a woman and a man meet, it is up to the woman to make the first move, and offer her hand. There is no hard and fast rule, however. If you feel like shaking hands, do so; it's a friendly gesture. But do it whole-heartedly: no one enjoys a limp handshake. Look directly at the person, not past him. Put some warmth into your voice when you answer, "How do you do?"—it helps remove any awkwardness in a situation.

(Shake hands wholeheartedly. No one enjoys coming in contact with a "limp fish".)

A man or boy always rises when introduced to someone. A woman or girl rises when the other person is older than she. A girl should rise always when parents walk into the room; a man or boy does the same and should also rise when a woman or girl comes into the room.

Correspondence

Many of us dislike writing letters even though everyone likes to receive them. By following some simple hints and rules about correspondence, you can avoid letting unanswered letters pile up and let answering them be a pleasure and not a hated chore.

There are various kinds of letters and notes you will need to write. Small, folded papers, called "informals" are most appropriate for several written responses. They are handy for answering invitations and for enclosing in gifts when you want to include a short note.

Be prompt with writing <u>thank-you-notes</u> for gifts or for hospitality. The paper you use depends on how much you intend to write. <u>Informals</u> may be used. The important thing is to put a little thought into your "thank you" and "bread-and-butter" notes. Show you really appreciate the other person's thoughtfulness by adding a personal touch to your note. Telling how you plan to use a gift, or how you will always remember the fun you had while visiting, will make the note more interesting.

<u>Invitations</u> sent by you need not be tricky or cute, but clear and direct. Give the what, when, where information and write RSVP in the lower left-hand corner if you want the person to reply. These initials are from the French phrase, Repondez, s'il vout plait, which means "please reply."

Edwardlene Fleeks Willis, Ph.D.

Answer all invitations promptly. Don't keep a hostess guessing about your response until the last minute. Answer all formal invitations on your best stationery in the third person or follow the form of the invitation.

Example:

> *Linda Woods*
> *accepts with pleasure.*
> *the kind invitation of*
> *Mr. and Mrs. Charles Edwards.*
> *to the marriage of their daughter Wanda.*
> *to.*
> *Robert Brown*
> *on*
> *Wednesday the twelth of June.*
> *at four o'clock*
> *The Mirage Hotel*

If you are unable to attend, you use the same form but say: "Linda Woods regrets that she is unable to accept..."

Condolence letters are an expression of sympathy for a friend's sorrow (usually the death of a family member), and are usually difficult to write. You can help ease the pain if you let a bereaved one know that you are thinking of him or her. Keep your letter brief, sincere, and simple.

There are no set rules for writing a friendly letter. Write as if you are talking to the person. Keep the letter chatty and newsy. Form isn't too important and an extra dash or exclamation point makes it more interesting. Avoid starting every letter with an excuse for not writing sooner, or end it with a "No more news - must stop now" ending. Before you write a <u>love letter</u>, a few words of caution: Stop and think how your feelings of everlasting devotion will sound several years from now. Don't overdo it!

In <u>personal correspondence,</u> put the date at the upper right corner of the sheet or at the bottom left below your signature. The year can be omitted. It isn't necessary to put your address on the letter, but always be sure it is on the envelope for the benefit of the post office and your friend who may have mislaid your address. Show concern for the postman and address your letters neatly and legibly.

<u>Business letters</u> have a different form and tone. State your business briefly and accurately. You can be cordial and at the same time impersonal. If possible, type your letter on plain, white bond paper, size "8-1/2 x 11". Your address and the full date go at the upper right corner. The person or firm to whom you are writing to on the left just above the salutation or at the bottom left below your signature. Type your full name underneath your handwritten signature.

Edwardlene Fleeks Willis, Ph.D.

Electronic-Mail System

This is an important medium for communication on the worldwide network. Electronic mail or e-mail is used by people of all age groups for educational, work related, and personal communication within the constraints of ethical standards and other policies, procedures, and job responsibilities.

Several points should be considered by e-mail users:

1. Electronic mail is private and owned by the sender and each recipient account holder. Electronic mail systems that are installed in the workplace should not be used by employees for personal communication.
2. The account holder is responsible for password security to maintain confidentiality in electronic mail. However, some systems have no such security measures.
3. The account holder is responsible for the management of her/his e-mail by suitably disposing mail in the account's mailbox. This includes saving documents and other information for storage in the computer's memory, printing messages, deleting messages and controlling automatic delivery of unsolicited bulk e-mail.
4. E-mail, telex messages, telegrams and mailgrams, are not transmitted on business letterhead. Also, instead of a traditional letter salutation and complimentary close, the memo format is used, with an abbreviated text. Practice editing electronic messages to reduce word length. <u>Examine the communications function:</u> List ways to avoid misunderstandings by making written and spoken messages clearer. Ask questions

Mind Your Manners
An Etiquette Guide for Youth and Young Adults

when you need more information and speak only for yourself, never for others without their permission.

E-Mail "Nettiquette"

This term means etiquette or good manners for the Internet. Some basic e-mail rules include:

1. Be polite. The absence of face to face communication doesn't give users a license to be destructive or rude. Being unable to "hear" a writer's tone of voice and double entendres can create misunderstandings and misinterpretations.
2. Type lower case. Typing in all caps GIVES THE APPEARANCE OF SHOUTING.
3. Edit before forwarding forwarded messages. It is rude to make the recipient wade through pages of forwards. Use your editing tools to cut and paste the message you are sending.
4. Refrain from using long signature blocks at the end of messages. Use no more than five lines.
5. Include question you are referencing when answering e-mails. Do not assume the recipient remembers what question you are referring to with your answer.
6. Keep e-mail conversational with shortcuts. Users express emotions and voice inflections through a combination of punctuation marks to create expressive faces and figures called "emotions", or "smileys". Two of the more commonplace ones are:

    Basic smiley for "happy" is**:-)**
    The smiley used for a tongue in cheek remark or "wink" is**;-)**

E-mail writers save space and time by using acronyms for typing shortcuts, although they are most commonly used in Internet Chat Rooms. Examples: **LOL**, stands for *laugh out loud;* BTW, *by the way;* IMP, *in my opinion;* and TIA is *thanks in advance.* Many more can be found at smiley web sites.

7. Beware of virus myths and hoaxes of the Internet. Always check for their authenticity. Legitimate companies do not conduct business via chain letters offering vacations, money, or class action checks. You won't have bad luck if you fail to send specified items to ten friends! There are no 'good times' virus. Many virus warnings are fabricated. Check them out before sending these e-mails that cause network congestion and work interference.

Voice-Mail System

A voice-mail system is a type of answering service. Instead of leaving a written message or PC-screen message (e-mail), voice-mail leave your spoken works to be retrieved bt the recipient at her or his convenience. An inhouse system requires computer controlled hardware and software that is linked to the telephone network. Local telephone companies also provide voice-mail services, and various message services are provided by commercial establishments. And commercial establishments provide various message services.

Voice-Mail Etiquette

Voice-mail systems, unlike paper or electronic text systems, have an added concern. It is the image that the spoken word conveys. Most rules of etiquette that apply to a telephone conversation apply to a voice message. For example, speak clearly and use a pleasant tone. This projects a gracious, professional image at all times.

Weekending

Weekending should be an enjoyable time for the guest and for the host or hostess. If you are entertaining someone for the weekend write and say what time you expect him or her, what your general plans are, and any necessary traveling instructions. You may consider including a timetable. If guests have some idea of the activities they will be doing, they will know what kind of clothes to pack. This information is extremely valuable for a female guest! Meet your guests at the station, and if the guest had a long trip, give him a chance to relax before involving him or her in any activities. Have the guest room-ready in advance and the bed made up with clean linen. Make the guest as comfortable as possible.

Clean towels, a book or magazine by the bed, a dish of fruit or flowers in the room, will show that you are trying to make your guest feel at home.

Introduce your guest to your family and friends. Include him/her In your conversations, so he doesn't feel like an "outsider". Your usual schedule of activities may be old and dull to you, but new and exciting to your guest. It is nice if you can arrange for some special activities during the visit, but you don't have to plan for every minute.

Family members are not expected to change their routine because of a houseguest. The guest will enjoy the family life, if there are no fights or arguments. This makes a guest very uncomfortable.

If you are invited to spend the weekend with a friend, all the responsibility for the plans and fun should not rest solely on the host/hostess. If your friend hasn't written you exactly when to come, write and give the time you are arriving and also when you are planning to leave.

Keep off your host's telephone. If you call long distance, use your credit card, or pay your host immediately.

It is thoughtful to bring a gift with you for your weekend host/hostess. It does not have to be fancy or expensive. If you prefer, you can send something that the hostess can enjoy after you return home.

Be a considerate guest and adapt yourself to the household schedule. If breakfast is served promptly at 8:00 a.m., be on time. Make your bed and straighten your room before you leave it. It will be greatly appreciated. Leave the bathroom tidy with no rings around the tub or wet towels on the floor.

Even if the planned activities are not exactly what you would choose to do, enter enthusiastically into all of them.
If there aren't any plans, inform the hostess that a quiet relaxing time was just what you needed and came for. To avoid being underfoot in the house, curl up with a book or go for a walk while your hostess is busy. If you act as though you are having a good time, you probably will! When you get home, write a sincere, warm thank-you note right away.

Driving Manners

The most important manners to mind are those needed behind the wheel. They involve not just courtesy and social success, but life itself.

Mind Your Manners
An Etiquette Guide for Youth and Young Adults

The number of traffic casualties is constantly rising, and the percentage of teenage accidents is shockingly high. Increase your margin of safety by driving carefully and courteously. The two go together.

The responsibilities of a passenger are:

-Don't talk on and on and divert the driver's attention.
-Don't say, "Oh, look at that ..."
-Don't crowd in as an extra passenger.
-Don't get coy or romantic.
-Don't be a back-seat driver.
-Don't ask, "How fast can this car go?"
-Don't say, "Let's beat that car"
-Don't ride with a driver who has been drinking.

(Driving manners are the most important of all)

The responsibilities of a driver are:

-Don't overcrowd your car.
-Don't mix romance and driving.
-Do slow down on sharp curves.
-Don't speed.
-Don't make dangerous "U" turns.
-Don't try to pass another car on a curve or a hill.

-Don't cross over into the wrong lane when passing.
-Don't let your attention wander from the road for even a moment.
-Don't "jump" the lights.
-Do obey all traffic rules; they are made for your safety.
-Don't drink and drive.

Cellular Phone Driving Tips

Many countries have banned the use of handheld phone while a vehicle is in motion. Check the laws and regulations on the use of wireless telephones in the areas where you drive. Always obey them. Also, if using your cellular phone while driving, please:

-Give full attention to driving! Driving safely is your first responsibility;
-Make sure the phone is easy to see and reach;
-Use hands-free operation, if available. Some cellular telephones are integrated into the dashboard of vehicles;
-Never dial your cell phone or take notes while driving;
-Let the cellular voice mail service take the call and listen to the message later, when you are parked, if the phone rings while you are driving;
-Let the caller know you are driving, if you must answer your cell phone. Suspend the call until you can pull over;
-Don't engage in stressful conversations that may divert your attention from the road;
-Pull off the road and park before making or answering a call if driving conditions are hazardous;

CHAPTER IX

BUSINESS ETIQUETTE

How to get a job and keep it are primary concerns of anyone planning to enter the business world. The most important thing about any job, whether it is part-time or a regular one, is that you do it well and conscientiously. Knowing your business etiquette is a vital part of getting and keeping any job. A prospective employer may decide against hiring you because you show an unpleasant manner. You may be fired from a job because you take too many breaks! In both instances, you would seldom be told why you did not make it on the job. In the first instance, the employer might say, "Try us again in a few weeks." In the second example, your employer might say, "You don't fit into our company." To avoid these and other pitfalls of the business world, check your business etiquette.

Applying for a Job

Writing a letter of application is one of the best ways to get more information about a job. It is also a good way to sell yourself. Your letter, if neat and informative, may lead to an interview and a job.

When writing a letter of application, follow these steps:

1. Typewrite or write legibly in ink only on one side of plain, white bond paper, 8-1/2"x 11"
2. Spell all words correctly. Use a dictionary to check your spelling. Make complete sentences punctuate accurately. Use the standard style of English

3. Keep your letter short, but include enough information about yourself to make someone want to know more about you.
4. State at least one good reason why you think you can do the job
5. Briefly describe your education and experience
6. Ask for an interview at which time you will give more details about your qualifications.

Here is a sample application letter written in answer to a newspaper ad for a nurse's aide.

1124 Lee Street
Crockett, Texas 75835

January 10, 2002

Carl Bunds, Personnel Director
Buchanan Nursing Home
P.O. Box 1195
Crockett, Texas 75835

Dear Mr. Bunds:

The January 9, 2002, Crockett Times listed your advertisement for a nurse aide to work in a convalescent home, I would like to apply for the job.

I am a May, 2000 graduate of Washington High School with a general academic diploma. I have just completed the training course for licensed vocational nurse at East Texas Community College and received a rating of Above Average. I can furnish character references and a letter of recommendation from my training supervisor. For the past two summers, I worked as a volunteer at the Sunset Retirement Village Clinic. I have a car in good condition.

I would appreciate an interview with you to discuss my job qualifications in greater detail. My telephone number is (214) 793-3257. I hope to hear from you soon.

Very truly yours,
Joan Pinch

A more complete method is to write a brief letter, and enclose an additional sheet, a resume, or personal information sheet, organized in five parts:

1. Address: Center your name, address and telephone number at the top
2. Personal Data: Age, height, health, marital status
3. Education: List most recent education first and continue in reverse order, make a complete record of all education and training you have received.
4. Experience: Give a brief history of your work experience, including employer's names and addresses, dates of employment, type of work done, and your income at each job.
5. Affiliations: List any job-related activities and volunteer work. If you have ever held a title or office, such as treasurer, secretaries, or president of any organization, list that first. This shows leadership qualities.
6. Personal Interests: List any hobbies or special interests that will help a prospective employer know something about you and might help you qualify for the job. This information is often used as an "ice-breaker" during an interview.

7. <u>References:</u> List references giving full names, address, telephone number and title, or position. Get their permission. Do not include relatives or former employers. They should be people who know the type of person you are.

Once the resume is completed, check your spelling and be neat. Ask several people to read the resume and tell you how it makes them see you. Add any of their helpful ideas and suggestions. Type the resume with black or dark-blue ink and center it on white or off-white paper with a one-inch border all around.

The Interview

Job applicants should be particularly careful and aware of their personal appearance and attitude because they are more easily observed and judged during the interview. The interviewer will be interested in your appearance, suitable clothing, personality, communication ability, manners, attitude and skills. If you are dressed neatly and appropriately, and have a positive attitude, you will be able to relax and make a good first impression when you talk with someone about a job.

Avoid any current fads that label you as a high school student rather than a prospective employee. This includes sloppy tennis, as well as over-baggy sweaters. If you expect to be paid for an adult job, look as though you are capable of handling one. A young man should wear a well-pressed conservative suit or slacks and a jacket so the interviewer can see him, and not a wild outfit. A clean shirt, polished shoes, a not too-flashy tie, and a recent haircut are needed for a businesslike appearance.

Mind Your Manners
An Etiquette Guide for Youth and Young Adults

A young woman should select an outfit that is a happy medium between school clothes and party outfits. It is just as inappropriate to be overdressed, as it is to give the impression that you are on your way to history class. Avoid jangling jewelry, complicated hairdos, heavy makeup, and fussy clothes. A simple suit with a fresh blouse, or a tailored dress is always appropriate for an interview. A simple handbag, gloves, and pumps will give you that well-put-together look. A light lipstick, powder, and a hint of cologne will help bolster your confidence.

Take your sample job application and other important papers with you. Know something about the firm or plant where you are applying. Pronounce the name correctly before you arrive for the interview. You can talk more intelligently and will have a better idea of how you might fit in as an employee. Your interviewer will be impressed to learn that you have taken the time to get this information.

Greet the interviewer with "Good morning/afternoon" or "How do you do?" "Hi's" and "hello's" are too casual. Sit still and erect and control fidgeting. If you are given an application form to fill out, do it carefully. Have a pen with you for this purpose.

The following tips will help you fill out an application form completely and accurately.

1. Read and follow the instructions and examples carefully.
2. Be neat. Print or write clearly so it can be easily read. Use a pen or type it.
3. Answer every question. If a question does not apply to you, write none or draw a line in the blank to show you did not overlook it.

4. Read everything on the application carefully before you start to fill the blanks. This will keep you from making mistakes. Be sure your spelling is correct. Have your personal information sheet or resume with you and refer to it for names, dates, etc.
5. Ask the person who gave you the application form about any abbreviations on the form if you do not know them.
6. List all types of education, experience, on-the-job training, or hobbies that have given you stills for any type of work.
7. Describe your previous work experience accurately and completely. Employers are looking for applicants with skills, abilities, and experience. List all of the different types of machines and equipment you have operated or can operate.
8. Include any special license, certification or membership in a trade union on the application form.
9. Take a personal information form and important papers with you when you go looking for a job or for an interview. They will save time and help you fill out the application completely and accurately.

During the interview answer all questions quietly and confidently. You can answer with more than one word, but avoid excessive chatter. The interviewer is interested only in pertinent facts and will be impressed by a pleasant, assured manner. Even though you are anxious for the job, don't seem too eager. Smile, but avoid being giggly or gushy. Tell the interviewer how your qualifications will fit the job, rather than why you want or need it. The interviewer is interested mainly in what you can do for the company—not in what the company can do for you!

When the interviewer indicates that the interview is over, rise and make your goodbye briefly. Thank the interviewer for his or her time and add one last plug for the job, as: "I am sure I could do an excellent job for you," if you feel that you still want the job. If you feel, during the course of the interview that you do not want the position, for whatever reason, say so immediately rather than wait until you are offered the job.

Keeping a Job

Getting the job is fine, but you want to keep it. This can be done if you are capable of doing the work efficiently. It is an important point in your favor after you are hired. However, there are many seemingly unimportant things that can make or break you on the job.

These are habits and techniques you should cultivate for success on a job. These come under the heading of good manners and includes:

1. Be on time or even a few minutes early. Give an honest day's work for a day's pay.
2. Always look your best.
3. Avoid being too familiar with your supervisor or boss.
4. Be courteous by treating others, as you would like to be treated.
5. Show respect for the knowledge and judgment of co-workers, especially those more experienced than you.
6. Know when to keep silent. Do not gossip or repeat anything that might hurt someone else.
7. Avoid out-of-place humor. There is a time and place for everything.
8. Be friendly and cheerful and do your share of work don't waste time on the job.

9. Do not make fun of others or laugh at their mistakes.
10. Be willing to help others with their work. But offer your help and suggestions only when they are needed.
11. Take care of your health.
12. Learn your employer's rules and follow them. Take an interest in your work.
13 Be honest.
14. Be neat and accurate with assigned tasks.
15. Be willing to get additional assignments, as necessary.
16. Avoid self-pity, grumbling and complaining.

Even though you have heard some of these things before, take inventory of your business manners once more.

		YES	NO
1.	Do you make personal telephone calls? They not only keep you from doing your work, but disturbs the whole organization by placing an added burden on the communication system.	____	____
2.	Do you practice good telephone manners? You serve as a good public relations person for your company if you answer the telephone in a polite, quiet voice, using whatever form your company requires.	____	____
3.	Are your lunch hours unpredictable? As soon as you begin work, settle with your supervisor on a convenient hour and stick to it. He or she will know when to expect you back at your workstation.	____	____
4.	Are you always away from your desk or workstation? Are you constantly in the rest room? Are you frequently going for coffee or a soft drink?	____	____
5.	Do you gossip or spread the office		

grapevine?
Magpies of both sexes are annoying in
any workplace, and particularly the
gossipy ones.

6. Do you keep your business life separate
from your social life?
Keep all your social activities until after
work hours.

The answers to questions 2 and 6 should be "yes" to 1, 3, 4, and 5,"no".

(Employees dislike gossiping around the office or taking too many breaks)

Other job nuisances and objectionable habits are bringing family problems to the workplace; constantly interrupting someone else to ask how a word should be spelled instead of using the dictionary, or swearing all the time.

Most of the following habits come under the heading of bad manners. You may not realize that you have some of them. If you do, make a sincere effort to eliminate these habits. Ask a close friend to check you against the following list and do the same for your friend:

1. Adjusting your collar, cuffs, or belt
2. Backslapping
3. Banging telephone receivers

4. Chewing and popping gum
5. Clearing your throat
6. Cracking your knuckles
7. Coughing or sneezing without turning your head and covering your
   mouth with a handkerchief
8. Dashing in and out of room
9. Drumming or tapping with fingers, toes or a pencil
10. Fussing with your hair
11. Playing with rings, beads, or other jewelry
12. Scratching your head
13. Slamming doors
14. Sniffling
15. Sucking your teeth
16. Whispering when others are speaking
17. Wrinkling your brows
18. Yawning

Certain simple rules of behavior apply on the job just as they do anywhere else - a pleasant voice, consideration for others, and a cooperative attitude. These things make up the basis of all-social behavior at home, school, work, or in public.

Baby Sitting

This job is being discussed separately because it is unique and so many teenagers engage in it. Taking care or someone else's child for any period or time is a big responsibility. Always make sure you know where to reach the parents and also a doctor if any emergency should arise. The main concern here, however, is the way you should act as a baby sitter.

Mind Your Manners
An Etiquette Guide for Youth and Young Adults

Parents usually give specific instructions on how to put the child to bed if he or she isn't already asleep when you arrive for an evening sitting. Follow these instructions to the letter. Do not let the child run wild or stay up late. During the hours while the baby sleeps you may get bored and restless. This is the time to complete school assignments or read that book or magazine you brought along. You may look at television, or borrow a book or magazine, if you have the parent's permission. You may knit or work on one of your models. This is the time to resist the temptation to call all your friends, discuss school and social activities. Treat your employer's house with respect. Don't go snooping! Another room may look inviting, but stay away from it. Don't read their mail. If letter writing is on your mind, don't use your employer's stationery. Bring your own. Leave the refrigerator strictly alone. If a snack has been left for you, your employer will tell you about it. Otherwise, hands off! Your employer's drawers, closets, perfume bottles, and so on, should remain untouched by your hands. You are on your honor to behave properly. Your employer has shown trust in you by leaving the place in your hands. Use your good, common sense. Behave, as you would like a stranger to act in your home.

Edwardlene Fleeks Willis, Ph.D.

CHAPTER X

TRAVEL ETIQUETTE AND TIPS

The universe is your oyster

Going from place to place is a great adventure or escape for neophytes striking out for the first time and for globetrotting veterans. Now that applications are being accepted for space travel from ordinary citizens, the universe is your oyster. Regardless of the purpose of your trip, travel offers one of the best outlets for youthful spirits, open-mindedness and recurrent pleasure.

Many tours are designed to introduce you to the people and cultures of different countries. When visiting other countries, you should be mindful of your manners. To fully enjoy overseas travel, remember you are visiting a different continent and each country on that continent has a unique set of people and a variety of customs. To help you avoid social and behavioral blunders, it is a good idea to be familiar with these customs. These include all the human activities of a country - or of the different groups within a country - such as using language, dining, dressing appropriately, getting married, rearing children, dating, earning a living, and taking part in recreational, educational, and political activities or religious ceremonies.

Outside the amenities of your hotel, you will find that many countries do not have the goods and services common in your home country. By experiencing or observing different standards of living of other societies, travelers are in a position to understand and appreciate the diverse cultures of the world. They also have the unique opportunity to become spokespersons and symbols of their country. They can do credible performances as "diplomats" by being adaptable, alert, outgoing and tactful. Francis Bacon wrote in Essays of Great Places, "If a man (woman) is gracious and courteous to strangers, it shows he(she) is a citizen of the world".

PLANNING AND PREPARING FOR YOUR TRIP

Traveling can be a smooth and enjoyable experience with careful planning. This effort is very worthwhile no matter how much time you spend on your journey. Following some suggestions of tips for travelers can greatly minimize any undue pressure leaving on a trip and during your journey.

Travel Agents

To help you select a reliable travel agent get a recommendation from a friend who has dealt with a particular agent or agency. Other sources for additional information about an agent or agency are the local Better

Business Bureau and the Consumer Affairs Department in the city or the State Attorney's Office, and the Internet.

With countless fare variations offered by airlines, land transportation services and cruise lines, plus hundreds of vacation options available today, it is wise to seek the services of a professional whose advice can often save you money on fare, lodging, excursions and some special sports activities.

Method of Payment

Usually travel tickets must be paid at the time of booking. Some tours and packages require a deposit with additional scheduled payments. Hotels often require one night's deposit. Most vendors accept credit card charging. Extended payments can be arranged on some credit cards.

Insurance

Liability and life insurance are provided by most credit cards when tickets are charged on the card. This coverage seldom extends to baggage or trip cancellation. These two types of insurance are strongly recommended and can be bought through your travel agent.

Travel Documents

Prior to departure, your travel agent should deliver three sets of documents to you.

1. <u>Tickets</u> - Check flight number, arrival, and departure times. Call immediately if there are mistakes.

2. <u>Travel vouchers</u> - For all ground reservations. Each voucher should give name and address of the hotel or

specific service you requested, your name, dates of arrival and departure, descriptive nature of reservations, rate in United States or local funds, amount of deposit, if any. Voucher should be presented on arrival.

3. <u>Itinerary</u> - Three copies of your complete itinerary are needed: One to take with you and one each for your home and office.

The itinerary should duplicate the voucher information, including meals served en route, hotel phone numbers, FAX numbers, Telex numbers and cable codes. Make sure you leave the name of the travel agency, contact person, and phone number with your home and office.

Agent should furnish you with specific suggestions and tips on dining, shopping, sightseeing guides and general touring information on each destination.

Overseas travel can be both exhilarating and exhausting. To help enjoy transoceanic flights and some domestic flights, ask your agent about non-smoking flights. Many airlines offer one or more international flights per week that are designated nonsmoking. Request a window seat if you plan to sleep so you'll have something to lean against. Aisle seats are better for roaming and leg room. Allow yourself at least 90 minutes if you must connect between a domestic and international night.

Passports

The United States Passport Agency maintains offices in all major cities. Check expiration date an your passport. Application for passports must be made in person unless applicant meets requirements established for securing passport by mail. To secure a passport by mail, obtain application and information from the local post office or country clerk's office. Allow sufficient time for processing. A fee is charged and passport photographs are required. An additional fee is charged by the agency for emergency service. If your passport is lost or stolen overseas, it should be reported immediately to the nearest United States embassy or consulate. Your passport number should be recorded and kept in a separate file.

To obtain a passport you will need the following:

Proof of Citizenship - This can be an expired passport, or certified birth certificate. If this is not obtainable, submit statements issued by appropriate authorities that no birth records exist and secondary evidence of birth in the United States is supported by a baptismal or circumcision certificate. Other documentary evidence created not more than 5 years after birth and/or affidavits of persons with personal knowledge of birth can be used as well. Those born outside the United States require certificate of naturalization or citizenship or naturalization certificate of parent, plus proof of blood relationship and date of entry into the U.S.

Photographs - for passport require two duplicates: 2" x 2", front view, full face, centered in print, head image 1" x 1 3/8" measured from bottom of chin to top of head (including hair) taken within six months. Black and white or color photos are acceptable.

Proof of Identity - is any document such as a previous passport, driver's license, certificate of naturalization or of citizenship, which contains the signature and either a physical description or a photograph of applicant.

Visas - A few countries require Visas for United States citizens. Some require only passports while others require proof of U.S. citizenship in the form of a copy of a birth certificate, or voter registration card. Visa applications are made to a country's embassy, consulate, or tourist board. Your travel agent can provide necessary forms and assist you. A fee is charged and passport type photographs are required.

Medical and Health Considerations

To help insure a pleasant trip without illness or mishap, follow these suggestions:

1. For places in the world that require immunizations shots, have your doctor administer proper dosages and give you a record of all shots or boosters. Secure copies of prescriptions you use in case you need medication. A brief, signed statement on treatment of any pre-existing condition would also be helpful.
2. Carry along a sufficient supply of regular medication and double the amount you normally would use, in case your return might be delayed or baggage lost. Put the extra amount in separate containers to minimize the change of loss.
3. Pack a second pair of eyeglasses.
4. Buy foam earplugs to help you sleep on a long flight.
5. Eat lighter meals before and during a flight to feel better when you arrive at your overseas destination. Call the airline and order a special meal, such as a fruit or vegetable plate. Pack raisins or crackers for the munchies.
6. Drink 8 to 10 glasses of water each day and reduce alcohol and caffeine intake. These measures help offset in-flight dehydration.

7. In the tropics, undeveloped countries, and remote areas, <u>do not drink tap water,</u> or use <u>ice cubes</u> in your drinks. Sealed bottled water or drinks reduce the risk of bad water from limited sanitation facilities.
8. Eat only those fruits you have peeled yourself unless you are staying in a four-star or better hotel where kitchen equipment and staff can be considered safe. Never buy juice or peeled fruit from a street vendor for personal consumption.
9. Avoid raw vegetables and salads.
10. Never eat raw or undercooked meat, raw fish, and undercooked fish, chicken, or eggs. Risky business!
11. Swim only in pools with chlorinated water. Don't swim in fresh water and avoid salt-water beaches near towns, which dump untreated sewage into the sea.
12. Avoid raw milk and other dairy products including cheese and ice cream.

Intestinal discomfort and serious illness can be avoided by following suggestions 7-12.

CUSTOMS AND TAXES

Foreign Customs

Be aware of foreign customs, especially if you are bringing in a gift to a resident of a country, or are carrying alcohol or tobacco products exceeding allowable limits. Many countries also have regulations regarding the amount of currency that can be brought in or removed. Have prescription drugs in their proper containers and have prescriptions for them.

Mind Your Manners
An Etiquette Guide for Youth and Young Adults

United States Customs

Facing a customs officer can cause even the most honest traveler some concern when asked about the value or origin of an object. A customs declaration form will be handed to you before landing and disembarking. If the value of purchases or gifts does not exceed the current exemption, only complete the identification section at the top of the form.

Duty Tax

Keep receipts of purchases handy for proof of payment. Try to pack all purchases in one bag. Don't bring back any fresh fruit, plants, flowers, fresh pork, or meat products or certain dairy products. The customs officer usually calculates duty, if any, on items carrying the lowest rate. Personal checks are usually accepted for duty payments.

Departure Tax

Many countries charge a departure and/or arrival tax or airport fee. Check with your travel agent to determine if this is included in the cost of your ticket. If not, be prepared to pay it on arrival and departure.

In-Flight Tips

Traveling by air can be both exciting and exhausting, especially overseas flying. The following pointers for pre-trip planning and the night itself can help you in the future:

1. Take a liter of boiled water to sip on a long flight so you won't have to rely on beverage service. It is recommended to drink 8 ounces for every hour you are in the air.

2. Consider packing a sweat suit in a carry-on bag to wear on board. Also pack the clothes, toiletries, and medication you will need for one day and night in case of lost luggage or flight cancellation. Change into your sweats after takeoff before the beverage and meal services begin. Just before arrival, change back into your traveling outfit, and dispose of any fruit, grains, or nuts. Most countries don't allow you to bring them in.
3. Take a good book to read. Bad weather, cancellations, and delays can add hours to a trip.
4. Arrive at the airport at least 90 minutes before departure to check baggage and confirm seat selection. If you have a pre-assigned seat from your travel agent, check with the gate agent anyway. You may get a better one.
5. Grab two to three pillows and a blanket when you board the plane. They will all be gone in an hour or less into the flight
6. Keep valuables or passport with you when you leave your seat. Do not leave important items in the seat-back pocket. They could be stolen.
7. Use moisturizer on hands, face, and neck every couple of hours for relief from the dry, re-circulated air on the plane. Atomizers are popular, but lotion works better.
8. Reset your watch on the plane. Start following your destination schedule as soon as possible. Take an alarm clock and set it for the morning after your arrival to avoid sleeping until your biological, normal "get up" time. Schedule tours, meetings (business traveler) when you would normally be alert; early morning for westbound trips or late afternoon for an eastbound trip.

Mind Your Manners
An Etiquette Guide for Youth and Young Adults

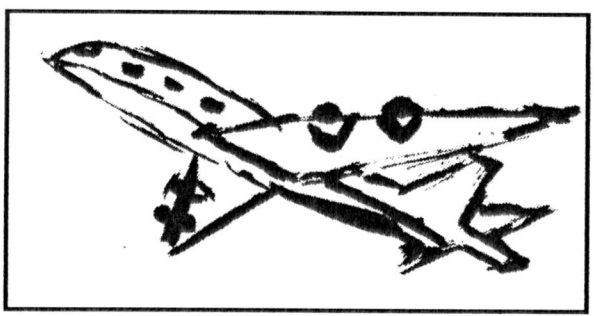

(Overseas Travel can be Exciting and Exhausting)

9. Beat jet lag to a great degree. Jet lag is the maladjustment you suffer after crossing time zones quickly. Symptoms include insomnia, sleepiness, fatigue, digestive problems, moodiness, lack of energy, and decreased alertness. Jet lag does not affect equally. Late-niters adjust better to jetlag. Younger people adjust better than older people. Research indicates that while jet lag affects stable extroverts less, sleep deprivation may cause manic or depressive episodes in some individuals.

    Check into your hotel after the flight. Though you may want to sleep, nap no more than two hours. Exposure to one hour of day light for each time zone crossed helps in quick jet log recovery.

    Because your body's internal clock runs slow, traveling westward (lengthening the day by losing an hour for every time zone crossed) is easier than traveling eastward (shortening the day by adding an hour for each time zone crossed). There are no quick and easy cures for jet lag. Maybe some day an anti-jet lag remedy will be available.

10. Remember an airline courtesy not generally advertised: If your flight is delayed a few hours, you may be able to get a free-meal voucher. If the flight is

postponed overnight and you are stranded, the airline will offer you vouchers for hotel and meals. Airlines are less generous for a delay because of bad weather. Still, it can't hurt to ask for compensation. **Caution:** if you miss a cruise or connecting flight with a different airline, your airline will not reimburse the financial loss. For this type of trip, schedule enough time to account for possible delays.
11. Communicate your fears if you are an "anxious night passenger". Meet the flight deck crew so you can put a "face" on voices talking on cabin announcements. Crews aware of anxious passengers usually make more announcements describing their route, warning of upcoming turbulence or explaining delays. Fearful fliers are usually highly intelligent, creative, and visual. They should get magazines with big splashy photographs and dramatic shapes as an effective diversion.
12. Keep your ears open if you suffer ear pain, which often occurs due to pressure changes during descent. Swallowing, chewing gum, or talking helps push the extra air in the middle ear through the eustachian tubes. Blocked Eustachian tubes due to colds, sinus infection or allergies can cause excruciating pain and hearing damage. If this is your situation, postpone your trip if you can.

CRUISE PLANNING

Vacations afloat are a popular mode of travel. Cruising provides all the elements of escape and adventure that most people seek when planning a vacation. Cruise lines have maintained an ambitious program of constructing new state-of-the-art vessels with added on-board features and choices of exotic destinations. These offerings tantalize veteran mariners and first time voyagers.

Over the years, cruising has changed considerable, with emphasis on comfort and recreation. The rigid caste system that ruled social life on the great ocean liners of the past has all but disappeared. Few vessels maintain the three-class method segregating travelers: first, cabin and tourist. Liners are floating resorts with facilities and haute cuisine menus available to all passengers regardless of their accommodations.

Selecting A Cruise

Major cruise lines offer trips as short as a few days to "around the world" journeys lasting six months or more. Longer cruises can be booked in segments allowing you to join the trip at a foreign destination and leave another port. Many ocean liners offer "Fly and Sail" packages for this purpose. Airfares in these packages are extremely reasonable.

If you do not purchase a cruise package, your cruise rate does not include air transportation, port charges, some sports activities, shore excursions, alcoholic drinks, ice cream specialties, a' la carte restaurant charges, tipping - plus personal items as laundry, photographs room service, medical services, phone cells and telexes. Be sure you know what your cruise rate includes before leaving port.

Hundreds of smaller ships sail the larger lakes, rivers, and inland waterways in the United States and abroad. You can select luxurious accommodations or opt for working on a schooner as part of the crew.

Edwardlene Fleeks Willis, Ph.D.

Theme Cruises

Some cruises feature shipboard activities and shore excursions built around a special interest area or avocation. Experts and specialists in the field are on board to conduct classes, give lectures and performances. Your travel agent or printed material on the theme cruises can give you information on the time allotted for these activities.

Cruise liners normally offer a wide range of shipboard activities even without special themes. These often include cooking demonstrations, wine tasting, craft workshops, fitness classes and even elementary language instruction. These activities are in addition to the usual sports and recreational facilities.

(Ocean Liners Are Floating Resorts)

Cabins and Staterooms

A selection of a cabin or stateroom is very important, as it will be your home at sea for a period of time. The type of accommodations depends on individual budget, i.e., size, deck level, and location (inside or outside cabins). Pictures in brochures, charts, and ship plans often distort sizes. A personal inspection before sailing is best, especially if you live close to the homeport of the vessel. You can usually arrange to look at cabins and other facilities while passengers are boarding. Check the size of beds and bathroom facilities. Beds are often narrow bench-type cots and bathrooms are often very small.

Dining at Sea

Most ships have one main dining room and provide two seating at each meal. Seating can be booked when you make your reservation or when you board the vessel. There is a special desk for this purpose. Book the second seating if you like to linger over your meal. If you like to eat early, select the first seating. You can also request a table for two, or join a larger group.

Cruises are known for excellent food service: often referenced to as "a movable feast". Most ships offer afternoon teas, buffets, midnight suppers, and snack facilities, besides daily breakfast, lunch and dinner.

Dress and Special Events

"Dressing" for dinner each evening at sea ended years ago. However, almost every cruise of at least a week's duration features a Captain's Cocktail Party the evening of the first full day at sea and the Farewell Dinner. For these events passengers wear formal attire. Tuxedos and suits for men and cocktail dresses for ladies are acceptable. Let good taste be your guide. At the Captain's Cocktail Party, you will meet the captain and his staff, and the ship's photographer will take your picture, which can be purchased before the end of the cruise. The longer the cruise, the more "dress" events or galas with set themes may be scheduled, calling for appropriate costumes. Often the ship's staff has costumes on board to outfit passengers, if they wish (This is optional).

Casual wear and swimwear are usually worn on the ship or in port. Whether you decide to bring casual and evening attire with you or buy these items on your cruise you also should probably include the following:

- Sun visor or hat
- Sunscreen
- Deck shoes/walking shoes for shore excursions
- An enjoyable book
- Sweater or light jacket

Tipping

On most voyages, tipping is still necessary. On some cruises you will be advised to tip in bulk in specified amounts. The money is then divided among the various service members.

The cabin steward and stewardess and dining room steward directly affect your welfare while at sea and should be tipped accordingly. Follow the suggestions of your tour material. Envelopes are often provided for tipping. Other tipping is a matter of personal preference or experience according to extra service rendered to you by a service crewmember.

Vocabulary of the Sea

To avoid being mistaken for a "landlubber", try to "pepper" your conversation with following words:

Aft - The general direction from wherever you are to the rear of the ship.
Berth - Where you and the boat rest.
Bow - The front of the ship.

Bridge - The Captain's domain atop the passenger section of the ship. It is the control room of the ship, and under certain conditions on appointment, can be made for a visit.

Bulkhead - Any wall or partition.

Deck - Any floor or level on a ship.

Forward - The general direction from wherever you are to the front of the ship.

Midship - The center of the boat

Overhead - The ceiling

Port - The left-hand side of the ship.

Posh - "Port Outbound, Starboard Home": The best accommodation on the shady, cooler side of the boat back in the days when Britannia ruled the waves and there was steady traffic between the British Isles and ports east of Suez.

Quay - The word for a pier or dock in certain countries

St Elmo's Fire - St. Elmo is patron saint of sailors and his "fire", caused by static electricity, can be seen at night atop the waves.

Starboard - The right hand side of the ship.

Stern - The rear of the ship

Weather Deck - A deck exposed to the elements.

Before-Leaving Reading

Reading about your destination before you leave home can increase your enjoyment of your trip. If you read about a culture before you find yourself in the midst of it, you'll learn and see because you will know what to look for, plan specific excursions of special interest to you and experience increased surprise when things turn out differently from how you pictured them beforehand.

Edwardlene Fleeks Willis, Ph.D.

Two types of pre-reading that experienced travelers recommend are **(1)** guides to help you use your time effectively and **(2)** background reading on your destination to lead you to a deeper appreciation of what you see. Two sources to contact for this type of information are the United States Government Printing Office: Superintendent of Documents and the State Tourist Offices and tourist offices of foreign governments maintained in the U.S. Addresses and phone numbers for these offices can be obtained from your travel agent/agency local library, and most travel journals.

(Reading About Your Destination Can Increase Enjoyment Of Your Trip)

Foreign Language Guidebook

Speaking a foreign language is the essence of sophistication. Learning a foreign language before you travel abroad is a guarantee to do the best shopping, in-restaurant ordering, meeting interesting people, and finding unique jobs. At least purchase a foreign language guidebook or dictionary to learn often-used words and phrases. A hand held electronic translator may be the best travel companion. It contains over a thousand words in each of the five languages: English, French, German, Spanish, and Italian. It also translates freely between all five at the push of a button.

Mind Your Manners
An Etiquette Guide for Youth and Young Adults

Some often used words and phrases are as follows:

FRENCH	ENGLISIH	ITALIAN
Oui	Yes	Si
Non	No	No
S'il vous plait	Please	Per favore
Merci	Thank you	Grazie
Bonjour	Good morning	Buon giorno
Bonsoir	Good evening	Buona sera
Au revoir	Good-bye	Anivederci
Enchante(e)	How do you do? Please to meet you	Molte lieto(a)
Comment allez-vous?	How are you?	Come sta?
Pardon	I beg you pardon	Prego
Parlez-vous anglais?	Do you speak English	Parla inglese?
Exrivez-le, s'il vous plat	Please write it down	Per favore me, lo scriva
Pouvez-vous me dire?	Can you tell me?	Puo dirmi?
Pouvez-vous m'aider?	Can you help me?	Puo aiutarmi?
Je cherche	I'm looking for	Cerco
J' ai faim	I'm hungry	Ho fame
J' ai soif	I'm thirsty	Ho sete
Je suis fatigue(e)	I'm tired	Sono stanco(a)
Je me suis perdu(e)	I'm lost	Mi sono perduto(a)
C'est tres important	It's important	E importante

GERMAN	ENGLISH	SPANISH
Ja	Yes	Si
Nein	No	No
Bitte	Please	Por favor
Danke	Thank you	Gracias
Guten Morgen	Good morning	Buenos dias
Guten Abend	Good evening	Buenas tardes
Auf Wiedersehen`	Good-bye	Adios
Sehr Erfreut	How do you do?	Encantado(a) de Conocerie

Wie geht es ihnen?	How are you?	Come esta usted?
Wie bitte?	I beg you pardon	Perdoneme
Sprechen Sie Enchisch?	Do you speak English?	Habla usted Ingles?
Schreiben Sie es bitte aif	Please write it down	Por favor escribalo
Konnen Sie mir sagen?	Can you tell me?	Puede usted decirme?
Konnen Sie mir helfen?	Can you help me?	Puede usted ayudarme?
Ich suche	I'm looking for	Estoy buscando
Ich habe Hunger	I'm hungry	Tendo hambre
Ich habe Durst	I'm thirsty	Tengo sed
Ich bin mude	I'm tired	Esto cansado(a)
ich habe mich verirrt	I'm lost	Me he perdido
Es ist wichtig	It's important	Es importante

Travel Journal/Diary

A travel journal or diary is designed to help you plan all three phases of travel: before, during, and after. Keeping a diary while traveling helps you remember your experiences after you get home.

A travel journal or diary is a valuable book to have: with you whatever your destination. It contains needed information, reference numbers and important points to help insure a carefree and memorable vacation. They include:

Currency conversion chart	Metric Conversion Tables
Diary and Photo Section	Packing Checklists
Duty-Free Information	Passport Information
Equivalent Sizes	Perpetual Calendar
First Aid Tips	Time Difference Chart
Foreign Language Phrase Guide	Toll Free Travel Information
Foreign Weather Chart	Travel Terms

Mind Your Manners
An Etiquette Guide for Youth and Young Adults

Government and State Tourist Office
International Dialing

Itinerary Planner

U.S. Area Codes
U.S. Consulates and Embassies
World Map to mark your route

Packing

Cruise ships and airlines allow passengers a certain number of pounds of personal baggage per person. You should check with the appropriate carrier. Excess baggage fees are expensive.

Many group tours allow only one suitcase and one small piece of hand luggage per person. On many tours, you may change hotels every night. Try to take <u>what you can carry</u>. (TIP: Insert a small size piece of luggage into a large piece and pack around it. Consider packing a folded canvas type piece of luggage, too. This allows you to have two extra pieces for your return. Tourist often make purchases overseas during their travels and need room in their luggage for new items.)

(Pack Lightly! Before Leaving Review Checklist of Things To Do)

Edwardlene Fleeks Willis, Ph.D.

Pack Lightly

Avoid carrying clothes and shoes that make you look good but serve no other purpose. Take layered clothing for changeable weather. Comfortable shoes are a must! Vacations or business travel often require a lot of walking. High heels, tight shoes, and exotic styles should be left in your closet.

Be sure that all baggage and personal belongings are properly insured. All suitcases should be securely locked. Hand-carry all medications, jewelry, fragile items, valuables, and important documents.

Packing Lists:

MEN

-Accessories (cuff links, tie clasps, jewelry, etc)
-Belts/Braces (Suspenders)
-Brush/Comb
-Cap/Hat
-Gloves
-Hair Conditioner/Shampoo
-Hair Dryer (with converter/adapter)
-Handkerchiefs
-Hosiery
-Jackets
-Manicure Set

-Overcoat or Topcoat
-Pajamas
-Rain Gear (light, folding)
-Robe
-Shaving Gear

WOMEN

-Accessories (jewelry, scarve caps, belts, etc)
-Blouses
-Brush/Comb
-Coat
-Cosmetics
-Dresses
-Extra pair of glasses
-Gloves
-Hair Conditioner/Shampoo
-Hair curlers
-Hair dryer (w/converter/adapter
-Jacket
-Jumpsuit
-Lingerie
-Manicure Set
-Pajamas/Gown

Mind Your Manners
An Etiquette Guide for Youth and Young Adults

-Shirts
-Shoes/Socks
-Slacks
-Slippers
-Sportswear/Equipment

-Sportscoat
-Suits
-Sweaters
-Swimming Gear
-Ties
-Toothbrush/Toothpaste
-Underwear
-Swimming Gear

-Purses
-Rain Gear (light, folding)
-Razor
-Robe
-Shoes (dress, walking, exercise)
-Shower Cap
-Skirts
-Slacks
-Slippers
-Sportswear/Equipment
-Suits
-Sweaters
-Toothbrush/Toothpaste

General (Men & Women)

-Address Book
-Batteries
-Binoculars
-Books (guide, phrase, other)
-Bottled water
-Calling cards
-Camera
-Cash
-Cleansing Tissue
-Credit Cards
-Films
-Flashlight
-Instant Coffee
-Itinerary
-Keys

-Map
-Mirror (folding)
-Passport
-Plastic bags
-Pocket calculator
-Reservations
-Sewing Kit
-Soap
-Tickets
-Travel Clock
-Travel Iron
-Traveler's Checks
-Vaccination Certificate
-Wash cloths
-Writing paper/pen

Health Kit

-Antihistamine
-Antiseptic
-Aspirin

-First aid guide
-Motion sickness pills
-Nasal decongestant

- Bandages
- Burn Cream
- Diarrhea remedy
- Extra Pair of glasses
- Sunglasses
- Sunscreen
- Thermometer
- Topical anti-bacterial
- Ointment or spray

Things To Do Before Leaving

- Take security measures or set burglar alarm
- Leave extra keys with a neighbor, family member, or a friend
- Leave copy of itinerary with office and family
- Stop mail and newspapers (or arrange for newspapers to be picked up)
- Store valuables in safety deposit box
- Purchase travelers checks
- Purchase small amount of foreign currency for each destination for immediate expenses such as transportation and tips
- Check on water and electricity
- Pay necessary bills
- Arrange for care of pets and plants
- Pick up dry cleaning
- Purchase extra film and batteries
- Tag all luggages on the outside and include an identification tag inside

Bartering

In many countries, bartering is a way of life. It is a social custom. You may barter (trade) your clothing, shoes, jewelry for similar items in many market places. It is strongly recommended that you pack items like radios with tape players for bartering. Polaroid prints from your camera are prized trade items! Other popular items for barter that you can purchase from your local discount stores are lipstick, fingernail polish, eye shadow, perfume scents, incenses, calculators, cotton panties, bras, candy, pens, pencils, and books. Children like school supplies and books. Youth and adults like jeans, tee shirts, and caps.

Edwardlene Fleeks Willis, Ph.D.

SUMMARY

It is important to learn the skills of social living. Getting along with family and friends, doing well in school, preparing for the future and enjoying dates are things that matter to most young people. One thing that will help you in these relationships is the use of good manners. They are not a guarantee of success but help make every situation easier and more pleasant.

Once you know what to do and how to act, you can face every situation as it comes and not worry about making a good impression. If you are relaxed, interested in other people and aware of their feelings and comfort, you are indeed mindful of your manners and on the way to being a social success!

Index

Air travel. See Travel Etiquette (In Flight Tips), 99-102
Babysitting, 90
Buffet, 36-37
Business Etiquette, 81-91; applying for a job, 81-94; the job interview, 84-97; keeping a job, 87-90
Cell Phone Driving Tips, 80
Cellular Phone Etiquette, 9
Checklist, 8, 14; 36, 46; 63-64; 88-89
Correspondence, 71-73
Cruises. See Travel Etiquette, 102-106
Customs, 2-3; 98-99
Dances, See Party Manners, 20-27
Dating Etiquette, 43-55; calling for a date, 24
Driving manners, 78-80
Electronic Mail (e-mail) systems, 74-75
E-Mail – "Netiquette", 75-76
Entertaining, 28-42; parties, see Party Manners
Etiquette; See specific headings; Definition, 1
Family Etiquette (Good manners at Home), 5-12; borrowing, 6-7; curfews, 9-10; dating, 10-11; neatness, 8-9; personal responsibility, 11-12; privacy, 6; self-control, 7; telephone, 9
Foreign words and phrases, 108-110
Host's responsibilities; 28, 29
Introductions, 69-71
Invitations, 69-71
Letter writing. See Correspondence
Manners, See Etiquette; and others; definition, 1
Party manners, 20-27; refusing a dance, 26-27
Public Etiquette (How to Behave in Public), 56-68; athletic events, 59; churches, 59-60; elevator, 62-63; escalator, 63; good manners with your gang, 64; movies, 56; performance, 57-59; smoking, alcohol and drugs, 64-68; vehicle, 60-62; shopping, 60
Restaurant rules, 51-52

School Etiquette (Good Manners at School), 13-19; auditorium, 16-17; cafeteria, 15; clothes, 18-19; corridors, 15; friends, 17; how to get along at school, 13-14; personal appearance, 18
Setting a table, 30-32
Table manners, 32-34
Telephone Etiquette, 9
Travel Etiquette and Tips, 92-115; bartering, 114-115; cruise planning, 102-106; customs and taxes, 98-99; flight tips, 99-102; foreign words and phrases, 109-110; packing, 111; packing lists, 112-114; planning and preparing for your trip, 93-102; 103-106; 111; vocabulary at sea, 106-107
Voice Mail Systems, 76
Voice Message Etiquette, 76-77
Weekending, 77-78

Authors Biography
Edwardlene Fleeks Willis, Ph.D.

Edwardlene Fleeks Willis is a consultant for social service organizations and educational institutions. Her career in education has included teaching high school mathematics, English, and business in Texas, Maryland, and Ohio, as well as serving as a school administrator. Recognition of the need for a handbook on etiquette and decorum for young people arises from these experiences as well as her early training at home and at Girls High School (San Francisco, CA).

Dr. Willis resides in Crockett, Texas where she continues to write and manage **Fleeks Farm**, registered in the *Texas Family Heritage Land Program.* This prestigious program honors farms and ranches, which have had continuous agricultural production for over 100 years in the same family. She is the widow of Dr. George M. Willis, a research scientist, and has two sons and two granddaughters.

The author gratefully acknowledges the assistance and encouragement of Josephine Morris, Clifford Pollard, Ph.D., Christine Martin, and her son Mirron E. Willis.

Printed in the United States
1172100001B/64-147